ONE MAN'S STRUGGLE WITH
OBSESSIVE COMPULSIVE DISORDER...

CROWD

ALONE
IN
THE

D1157157

JOE H. VAUGHAN

FOREWORD BY
JOHN J. O'HEARNE M.D.

ii

Dedication

To my parents...
Joe H. Vaughan (1904 – 1966)
Elizabeth W. Vaughan
...*without whom I would not be*

To my daughter...
Lauren Elizabeth Vaughan
...*the light of my life*

Joe Vaughan Associates
Communications Services and Publishing
P.O. Box 8524
Prairie Village, Kansas 66208-0524

Library of Congress Catalog Number: 566 369 (Form TX)
ISBN: 0-9636863-6-4
Printed in the United States of America
FIRST EDITION 1993

AUTHOR'S PHILOSOPHY

based on his real life experience...

"One's life is pretty much cast to fate...
and fate is a most cruel and
unyielding negotiator."

— **Joe Vaughan,**

in the depths of a personal crisis in 1977

Contents

Foreword

by John J. O'Hearne, M.D.

This book is about Obsessive-Compulsive Disorder (OCD). It contains the story of one man, Joe Vaughan, as he struggled against the disease. These struggles go back to the time when he was eight years old. As his symptoms became clearer, his parents tried everything. They took him to an older pediatrician, a partner to his late maternal grandfather, Dr. Hugh Wilkinson, a surgeon. He tried Serpasil. The first psychiatrist tried Donnatal liquid and Elixir Alurate; the next tried sodium amytal and Thorazine. Joe tried Valium and, when that was thought to be addictive, he was switched to BuSpar and then to Ativan. You may think we didn't know what we were doing. We could control some of the tension, but we couldn't control the brain.

People with OCD may hurt themselves, but NEVER others. Joe's appearance and demeanor leave nothing to be desired. You would pass him in a crowd without noticing him. Testimony to his diligence is the fact that he has never missed more than four or five days of work since he graduated from the University of Kansas in 1971.

For a long time, the manifestations of OCD were thought to be psychological. Now we recognize that many of them come from the brain and can be largely controlled with Prozac. That has been a wonder drug for Joe. It does nothing for his uncontrolled anxiety he feels when working in close quarters around people or when having to conform to someone else's time schedule.

A few doubters say Joe could control his symptoms if he wanted to. I say he cannot. And I've known Joe for a long time — since 1964. I've seen him grow up from a boy who couldn't stay in school for conviction that he was going to sit in an electric chair, not an ordinary classroom; from a frightened boy to the man who was chapter advisor for his fraternity; from the hopeful young man who married, to the man who came home one day to find his furniture moved out and his wife and child gone.

There are unexpected islands of disease intermingled with his mainly superb performance. He can't tell when they will surface; neither can we. No one can explain why the person with OCD has some symptoms of the disease and not others. Joe is among the approximately 5 million Americans, or 2% of the population, who have this disease.

Group therapy in two different groups failed him (I am past president of the American Group Psychotherapy Association). We have left what he started with, individual psychotherapy, but we have hope now, with Prozac, that he will be able to continue the tradition of his paternal grandfather, the late W. Lee Vaughan, Sr., who was a prominent druggist and theatre owner whose philanthropy included underwriting soup kitchens for churches and the Salvation Army during the Great Depression, and his parents, both well-known area civic leaders in their own right.

John J. O'Hearne, M.D.
Kansas City, Missouri
December, 1992

Preface

It's a lot easier to just say and hear the good things about yourself. But we often learn the most from the experiences in life that were NOT so good. *Alone in the Crowd* is written for the learning experience of those many other people who have had similar experiences to mine but thought that surely no one else in the world was like they. And, it is written in the spirit of the Greek philosopher, Sophocles, who wrote: "There is no success without hardship."

I have been under treatment for Obsessive-Compulsive Disorder/Anxiety Disorder (OCD) since I was eight years old, although doctors did not have a name or category for my well-defined symptoms for the first 31 years. OCD was not officially identified by the medical and scientific communities until 1987. There are numerous and insightful books and other publications about OCD written by researchers, academicians, doctors and others. However, *Alone in the Crowd* may be the initial first-person, public look at the disease, what it is like and how to cope and function with it in the everyday world.

Hopefully, my story will lead to a greater understanding among the general public and offer insight and hope to other OCD victims, their families, coworkers and others who may have regular contact with the two percent of the U.S. population who suffer from this disorder.

The title of this book comes from two thoughts. First, as one reads the material and the information it imparts, remember that only three or four people at any one time over a period of more than three decades ever knew what each day of my life was like.

Thus, I REALLY WAS ALONE IN THE CROWD.

Second, as a broadcast journalist for many years, I was in a small room by myself with only a microphone, tape player and control board while delivering newscasts to tens of thousands of people over radio stations in the Greater Kansas City area who could not see me or talk back to me while hearing me anchor the news. The paradox of intimacy and distance that is radio truly put me *Alone in the Crowd.*

DO NOT GIVE UP!! Whatever you do, whether you are an OCD victim or close to someone who is, do not give up on yourself or the relative or friend you are supporting. The late Helen Keller, American writer and educator, wrote: "When we do the best that we can, we never know what miracle is wrought in our own life, or in the lives of others." Keller, blind, deaf, and dumb, is the personification of perseverance for her incredible achievements.

Joe H. Vaughan
Prairie Village, Kansas
December, 1992

1

Introduction/Overview

Life is living Hell! It is for those with Obsessive-Compulsive Disorder (OCD) and the related Generalized Anxiety Disorder. Each day, the sufferer faces a fiery abyss of painful thoughts and convoluted and confusing emotions. The fear and embarrassment one goes through trying to hide the affliction from friends and coworkers drains the victim's energy and productivity in both work and leisure activities. The depth and intensity of the misery cannot be fully understood by those who have not experienced it themselves. Research conducted by the Obsessive-Compulsive Disorder Foundation, headquartered in New Haven, Connecticut, estimates that more than five million people in the United States have one or more identifiable symptoms of OCD. But most practice denial or try to cover up their symptoms out of fear of rejection or that their employers would fire them. Both of these afflictions are classified as multidimensional disorders.

I am a college-degreed professional man who has achieved considerable success over the last two decades in broadcast journalism, an intensely competitive business. My accomplishments include being news director, editor, anchor and reporter on highly-rated stations in a top-25 broadcast market. In addition, I have held leadership positions in several key trade associations, community service and fraternal organizations. These successes did not come without a constant struggle to overcome the tumult and turmoil caused by OCD and Anxiety Disorder.

The realities of life hit me hard and early, destroying my teenage years. Although not officially diagnosed with OCD until 1987, I suffered severe and debilitating symptoms as far back as 1961 (age 13) and symptomatic patterns of Anxiety Disorder dating back to 1956 (age 8). There was an extended period of virtual total dysfunction in the early years of the illness.

I grew up in a blue-collar, lunch-bucket industrial center in the Midwest. The city of 168,000 (1970 U.S. Census) comprised about 15 percent of the population of a major metropolitan area. I have no doubt that, if my family had not been prominent (my father was a retail merchant, banker, school board member and civic leader; my mother was a noted professional concert soprano and community worker), I would have been classified as an undisciplined malcontent in junior high school and either kicked out of the school or sent to an institution for such "incorrigible" teenagers. If that had occurred, there is no way to speculate on what my eventual fate might have been, other than to assume the worst case scenario as the most likely outcome.

For example, my dysfunction was so overwhelming that I was unable to sit in a classroom from the second semester of the seventh grade (age 13) until the second semester of my sophomore year of high school (age 16), a period of three years. At that point, I was able to return to school on a three-hour-a-day schedule following intensive twice-a-week counseling with a Presbyterian minister (Rev. Roy W. Pneuman), whose combination of strength and kindness gave me the self-confidence to leave a shadowy existence in lonely isolation and move toward the mainstream and leadership roles in the spotlight.

I told my psychotherapist that, among my many symptoms, I felt terrified approaching a seat in a classroom because it was like having to sit in an electric chair; I had a gaggy, short-breathed, cold, sweaty palms, panicky feeling that I had to get out of there fast, before something unknown and awful happened to me. As a teenager, I often described my feelings as "nervous nausea." My feelings of terror were truly irrational, but very real and frightening to me. In this period of my life, I was so plagued with a daily routine of rituals and obsessions that consumed most of my time and energy that I did not even want to socialize with other teenagers.

I remained on that limited schedule during my junior and senior years of high school and earned enough credits for graduation through a homebound study program. A humanitarian head football and baseball coach (the late Ed J. Ellis) allowed me to set my own schedule and work at my own pace as a student manager for his teams each fall and spring. That experience provided daily social contact with my peer group although the relationships were at a distance and superficial.

In the next few years, miracles would occur that will be detailed in later chapters. Intensive psychotherapy, new medications, lots of prayer and an indomitable "give 'em Hell" spirit enabled me to earn a liberal arts degree from a two-year community college and a BS degree in journalism from the University of Kansas, whose journalism program was considered to be in the top ten in the country at that time. Equally miraculous, after years of social isolation or near isolation, I became a popular leader in one of the university's most competitive men's fraternities. That experience laid the groundwork for many of my most successful and enduring relationships in both my personal and professional life.

Winning a reverse discrimination lawsuit can be considered one of my greatest victories. A major market radio station fired me in 1979 alleging verbally that there were deficiencies in my "air sound," but then gave a different reason for the termination in writing. My attorney stated in a petition filed in 1980 that I had actually been terminated because I was white. There was considerable factual evidence cited to back up the contention. A jury agreed following a week-long trial in 1983. The state court of appeals upheld the jury's verdict. And so did the state supreme court in 1986. It was not only important for me to win this case to preserve my career and livelihood, but it was vital to me as an OCD/Anxiety Disorder patient to remove any doubt about the real reason for my firing. Race was not the motivating factor; clearing my name and preserving my hard-won professional credibility were.

My wide range of personal experiences has given me unusual insight into the problems many contemporary youth have in coping with the demands of the classroom and society in general. I believe that a significant number of teenagers today may have OCD, Generalized Anxiety Disorder or other similar definable afflictions, but are never diagnosed or treated and drop out of school, ending up involved in a life of crime and drugs on the streets. These people end up in jail, other institutions or dead as their lives spiral downward. This could be one possible explanation for some of the problems now claiming large numbers of youths in both urban and suburban neighborhoods.

Urgent action must be taken. A mechanism could be added to the state-mandated student health care systems already in place in most of the 50 states to locate these troubled individuals in their pre-teen years so they can be treated and, hopefully, salvaged for a productive role in society. The cost of such an effort in relation to its potential benefit would be minimal because most of the essential apparatus already exists. I was very lucky to come from an enlightened family which sought and could afford professional help for me.

My treatment through the 1960s and '70s was compromised considerably by the lack of knowledge about what I was actually suffering from and how to effectively treat it. Today, there are methods of treatment available if the victims can be screened out when they enter junior high or middle school as a part of the existing health care system.

Coping with OCD can be every bit as difficult for its victims as the other so-called "major cripplers," including multiple sclerosis, muscular dystrophy, cerebral palsy and, in earlier years, polio. The difference is that effects of OCD are not usually visible and obvious like the illnesses mentioned. This fact results in even greater frustration for the OCD victim because the support and understanding given to the other victims are never there for an "invisible" or "masked" affliction. There's another factor that isolates OCD/ Anxiety Disorder patients even more tragically. It's the continuing attitude of avoidance many in society still have toward people with mental or emotional illness. The mere rumor that a person has seen a psychiatrist will frequently lead to that person's exclusion or isolation, a form of discrimination or prejudice.

Prominent people throughout history are believed to have suffered from OCD, the "secret" illness. The famous include John Bunyan, English novelist who penned *The Pilgrims Progress*; Samuel Johnson, another major English writer; and religious reformer Martin Luther. A more contemporary figure, the late billionaire Howard Hughes, was an OCD victim.

I could not have accomplished what I have without the strength gained from my Christianity. I grew up in the Presbyterian Church and am now a member of the United Church of Christ. I cannot count the times I have seen God working in my life. Let me illustrate it this way: Have you ever thought about the wind? You can feel it. You cannot see it or control it. But it is there and it is very powerful!

This book is not a medical publication or a how-to book. It is an informational book to inspire and guide others who have OCD and to inform and enlighten relatives, friends and co-workers who must be in regular contact with these people. It is also a tell-all celebration of my considerable personal and professional achievements assembled here to, hopefully, encourage others who may feel their life is doomed because of their affliction. It is written in layman's language by one who fought a desperate, lonely battle to be accepted as "normal" and has largely succeeded. The subsequent chapters will define OCD, Generalized Anxiety Disorder and their symptoms as well as relate my bitter battle to survive. Remember, for you, this is a story. For me, it was real life!

2

Defining Obsessive-Compulsive Disorder and Generalized Anxiety Disorder

Psychiatric diagnosis in the United States usually follows the rules laid out by the American Psychiatric Association (APA) in the *Diagnostic and Statistical Manual of Mental Disorders* (DSM). The APA periodically revises its DSM. Presently, the *Diagnostic and Statistical Manual of Mental Disorders, Third Edition, Revised* (DSM-III-R) is in use. Although the illness has probably changed little, mental health professionals are constantly updating the definitions of diagnoses as more facts are learned through research. The process will continue to be ongoing.

DSM-III-R defines OCD: "The essential features of Obsessive-Compulsive Disorder are repeated obsessions or compulsions, not necessarily both, that are significantly distressing or time consuming or that cause significant interference with social or occupational functioning."

Either obsessions OR compulsions are enough to make a diagnosis. The majority of sufferers, however, have both.

Obsessions are defined by DSM-III-R: "Obsessions

are persistent ideas, thoughts, impulses or images that are experienced, at least initially, as intrusive or senseless."

Compulsions are defined by DSM-III-R: "Compulsions are repetitive purposeful and intentional behaviors that are performed in response to an obsession, according to certain rules, or in a stereotyped fashion. They may be designed to neutralize or to prevent discomfort or some dreaded event or situation."

Generalized Anxiety Disorder is defined by DSM-III-R: "The essential feature of Generalized Anxiety Disorder is unrealistic or excessive anxiety or worry about two or more life circumstances for six months or longer, during which the person has been bothered by these concerns more days than not."

I have both obsessions and compulsions and Generalized Anxiety Disorder. At times, they affect me separately and, at other times, they function in tandem. The degree of each fluctuates constantly and is very unpredictable. These factors make the initial diagnosis extremely difficult and the ongoing treatment erratic in its effectiveness.

Other publications go into the above information in more detail, but the previous data set forth the premise to explain what has been happening in my life since 1956.

Researchers are reporting important new findings and confirming earlier theories about OCD at an increasingly faster rate.

A. D. Rasmussen and J. L. Eisen of the Department of Psychiatry and Human Behavior at Brown University said in the April 1991 edition of the *Journal of Clinical Psychiatry*: "OCD is now recognized as a common psychiatric disorder in the United States. The lifetime prevalence of 2% to 3% found in the U.S. has also been found in epidemiological studies in several other countries of diverse cultures." Rasmussen and Eisen add: "Depression and other anxiety disorders frequently co-occur with OCD, which may contribute to misdiagnosis." In the same edition of the same publication, J. H. Griest of the Department of Psychiatry at the University of Wisconsin stated: "The combination of behavior therapy and a potent serotonin uptake inhibitor is currently the best treatment for most patients. Psychosurgery still has a part to play in the treatment of a small portion of severely disabled and distressed OCD patients unresponsive to other effective treatments."

Another opinion from J. L. Rapoport, S. E. Swedo and H. L. Leonard in the same April 1991 publication revealed: "Childhood OCD has been recognized as being more common than previously believed, supporting epidemiological studies in adults that found rates far higher than clinical studies have suggested." Rapoport, Swedo and Leonard are with the Child Psychiatry Branch of the National Institute of Mental Health.

Researcher M. S. George of the National Institute of Mental Health reported in the December 1991 edition of the *International Clinical Psychopharmacological Journal* that: "Although the aetiology of OCD remains unclear, recent neuro-imaging studies implicate the basal ganglia and frontal cortex as crucial structures in the pathogenesis of OCD."

"Recent evidence now suggests that OCD is much more common in young people than previously thought, affecting up to 200,000 children and adolescents in the

United States alone." That research data came from
researchers J. Piacentini, M. Jaffer, A. Gitow, F. Graae,
S. O. Davies, D. Del Bene and M. Liebowitz of the College of Physicians and Surgeons of Columbia University writing in the March 1992 edition of *Psychiatric
Clinics of North America.*

G. W. Grumet of the Department of Psychiatry at
the Rochester (NY) General Hospital said in the February 1991 edition of *Psychological Reports* that,
"...many of the unwelcome features of modern life lead
to the increasing influence of obsessional traits. This
influence is becoming more pronounced as civilization
advances and comes to be increasingly reliant upon
depersonalized mechanical and commercial systems.
The result has been a glut of unwanted information,
an exaggerated reliance upon computing and numbers,
an overgrowth of bureaucracy, a discarding of intui-
tive wisdom in favor of calculative reasoning, a loss of
simplicity, a jargonized language and ultimately, the
degradation of human relationships and of human
beings themselves."

In the August 1990 edition of the *Journal of Clinical
Psychology*, J. H. Griest of the Department of Psychiatry at the University of Wisconsin stated: "Ninety
percent of obsessive-compulsive patients can be helped
by treatment with behavior therapy and drug treatment, used sequentially or concurrently. The effectiveness of these treatments has been demonstrated in
controlled clinical trials and is superior to electrocon-
vulsive therapy and dynamic or cognitive psychothera-
pies for this disorder." Although medications currently
available "usually do not induce complete remission,
they can reduce obsessive-compulsive symptoms by
30% to 42%."

Harvard Medical School's A. Rothenberg reported in the September 1990 edition of *Psychiatric Clinics of North America* that: "Although it is widely recognized that eating disorders primarily begin during the adolescent period, the centrality of obsessive-compulsive symptomatology and dynamisms and their relationship to adolescent conflict and development has not been generally accepted or understood. Social pressures toward conformity with the ideal of feminine thinness, which are especially influential during the adolescent period, combine with obsessive-compulsive predispositions to produce eating disorder symptoms and patterns of behavior. Obsessive preoccupation with images of food, use of laxatives and vomiting, together with an underlying focus on control, undoing and other obsessive-compulsive defenses, and a sado-masochistic orientation to the body all point to an essential obsessive-compulsive disorder." Rothenberg concludes: "Therefore, the current eating disorder picture appears to be a modern form of obsessive-compulsive illness beginning during the adolescent period."

In the *American Journal of Psychotherapy*, July 1990 edition, V. Starcevic of the Department of Psychiatry at the Belgrade University School of Medicine in Yugoslavia said: "...the relationship between obsessive-compulsive disorder and hypochondriasis can basically be conceptualized along the severity continuum so that hypochondriasis would be conceived of as a more pervasive and more incapacitating form of the same or closely related underlying psychopathology. The principal components of the psychopathology common to both disorders are perception of excessive threat to oneself with the consequent experience of vulnerability and insecurity, mistrust in oneself and others, greatly increased need for control, inordinate search for security, poor tolerance and fear of uncertainty and ambiguity and specific cognitive style, mainly developed to support a struggle for control."

E. Hollander, M. R. Liebowitz and C. M. DeCaria said in the Winter 1989 edition of *Psychiatric Developments* that: "An association between recurrent motor and phonic tics and OCD behaviors has been noted since Tourette's Syndrome was first described. OCD until recently was considered a rare disorder with poor prognosis. Currently, OCD is considered among the most common psychiatric diagnoses and new treatments have spurred the Chapter development of considerable clinical, epidemiological, genetic and biological research. Recent studies suggest a high rate of OCD symptoms in Tourette's Syndrome patients."

In the *British Journal of Clinical Psychology*, September 1989 edition, Cohen S. Baron of the Department of Psychiatry at the University of London said autistic children "are frequently reported to show obsessions and compulsions. This terminology implies that such behaviors in autism are similar to those seen in obsessive-compulsive disorder. However, these autistic behaviors fail to satisfy the definitions of either obsessions or compulsions because essential subjective data (relating to unwantedness, distress, resistance, senselessness and egodystonia) are not available in the case of autistic children." "...autistic children are unable to contemplate or talk about their own mental states." In this paper, "...the term 'repetitive activities' is used. To gain a better understanding of such repetitive activities in autism (more) functional analysis are needed." This is considered a neglected area of research.

Is OCD a genetic disorder? Many researchers believe that it may be. One of them, David L. Pauls, Ph.D., Yale Child Study Center, Yale University School of Medicine, addressed the question in the *OCD Newsletter,* Volume 3, Number 3, 1989:

"Several very interesting studies have suggested that specific regions of the brain may be involved in the illness and this, in turn, has led to hypotheses about biological factors being very important.

"The possibility that biological factors may be involved in the etiology of OCD suggests that genetic factors may also be important in the expression of the disorder. Relatively few studies have been undertaken to determine if genetic factors are important.

"However, these studies give some evidence that genetic factors do play a role in the expression of OCD.

"Several twin studies have been completed which suggest that OCD is inherited. The basic premise of twin studies is that if genes are important in the expression of the disorder, then monozygotic twins (MZ) (i.e., identical twins) will more often have the same diagnosis than dizygotic twins (DZ) (i.e., fraternal twins) because MZ twins are genetically identical and DZ twins are not.

"In all of the twin studies which have been reported for OCD, MZ twins are significantly more likely to both have OCD when compared to DZ twins. Thus, these data support the hypothesis that OCD is inherited. However, the specific genetic mechanism has not been determined.

"In addition to twin studies, family studies can give evidence that genetic factors are important for the expression of an illness. Studies of families can also provide data which are helpful in understanding the specific mode of inheritance of an illness.

"Several small family studies have been reported in which the rate of OCD among the first-degree relatives (i.e., parents, siblings, or children) was presented. In these studies, the results suggest that OCD is familial. That is, the rate of OCD among the first-degree relatives is significantly higher than the frequency in the general population.

"These family study results, when taken together with the twin study findings, suggest that genetic factors are in part responsible for some of the cases of OCD. These family studies have been too small to begin to study the mode of inheritance of OCD; therefore, we do not yet know the specific ways in which genes are involved in the manifestation of OCD. However, more extensive family studies currently underway should provide some data which will help to understand more completely the specific mode of inheritance of OCD.

"This work on the inheritance of OCD comes at an extremely exciting time in the field of human genetics. Research methods have been developed that make it possible to determine the actual chromosomal location of genes responsible for specific illnesses.

"For example, the gene for Huntington's disease (a progressive neuro-degenerative illness) has been localized to the short arm of chromosome four. In addition, a gene for Alzheimer's disease (a disease which is characterized by short-term memory) has been located on chromosome 21, and a gene for manic depressive illness has been found on the X chromosome.

"Given the findings discussed above with regard to the genetics of OCD, it is appropriate to begin to use the new DNA techniques to search for the gene, or genes, responsible for OCD.

"In order to do so, however, very special families are needed.

"First, these families need to have several members (four or more) who have a diagnosis of OCD.

"Second, there should be at least three living generations.

"And, finally, these families should be large: there should be at least 25 living members willing to participate.

"Participation in a study like this would require that each family member would be asked to give approximately two ounces of blood so that their DNA could be studied.

"If families such as those described above are available, the new genetic methods could be used to begin to search for the genetic factors involved in the manifestation of OCD. After the gene, or genes, are localized, the next step would be to determine what those genes do. If that is possible, then much more effective treatment could be developed.

"This is a long process, and will require a lot of hard work. But if there are genes responsible for OCD (and many people believe there are), these techniques should make it possible to find them."

The OCD puzzle will continue to be a difficult one to piece together. However, the process can be accelerated if more people who are afflicted come forward and discuss their symptoms so that their individual cases may be studied to further unravel the secrets of the secret illness.

3

OCD/Anxiety Symptoms Defined: How Each Affected Me

Deep, personal feelings and the unpleasant experiences that occur in one's life are hard for most people to talk about openly. One reason may be that the desire to find empathy is overwhelmed by the fear that rejection will come by disclosure. Even writing this chapter takes considerable courage. However, those who suffer with Obsessive-Compulsive Disorder may be relieved to discover that they are not alone (and that there can be better days down the road). For family, friends and co-workers of the afflicted, there is information which may increase understanding of the illness and the grief it brings. Some OCD sufferers are relieved to find some humor in their otherwise "ridiculous" thoughts. If even one person is helped by reading this, my effort will be completely rewarded.

The reader can determine if and how each of the symptoms relates to his/her situation as I describe my experiences with each one of them. In my case, the symptoms would surface both individually and in groups. Sometimes a symptom would disappear for a lengthy period of time only to reappear unexpectedly. At other times, multiple symptoms would be experienced simultaneously. The intensity level of each would vary with each occurrence and each combination of occurrences. The pervasiveness of the affliction is what makes it so devastating. Psychiatrists say that no two individuals would have exactly the same experience with any of the symptoms listed. Here, I have only defined and/or explained the symptoms I have personally experienced. The information in this chapter is intended only to inform and enlighten the reader and is not meant to be used for either diagnosis or treatment. Persons needing additional advice or interpretation based on this chapter should consult a psychiatrist or the nearest city or county public mental health office. It is the complexity of this disease that made treatment by my pediatrician, family physician, and psychiatrist, John O'Hearne, M.D., so difficult.

It is important for the reader to note that, while some potentially horrible scenarios will be described in this section, the OCD victim never acts out his/her obsessions or compulsions. They **fear** acting them out, but **never** actually do so.

AGGRESSIVE OBSESSIONS

Fear of Harming Yourself
I did not have this symptom. *

Fear of Harming Others
I did have this symptom. For example, I would be talking to someone in a one-on-one conversation and fear that at any moment I might suddenly double up my fist and punch the individual in the face. The individual's age, sex, race, size and the topic of discus-

sion were not factors. This could occur in either a work or social situation. It was very difficult for me to concentrate on the conversation because I was so distracted by the obsession. I had almost unbearable anxiety build ups in these situations because I wanted to leave or escape, but had to mask the feeling by smiling and appearing to be happily engrossed in the chat. The anxiety symptoms would vary, but usually came on suddenly and unexpectedly and included a short-breathed, gaggy feeling (like having a tongue depressor shoved down your throat) and/or a shaky, light-headed feeling with cold, sweaty palms. Frequently, the anxiety attacks culminated with a bout of abdominal cramps and diarrhea. I was troubled with chronic flatulence for many years.

Trouble with violent or horrific images

This symptom is what caused the distraction described above.

While battling the obsession, I would already have the image of the person I was talking to in my mind's eye lying on the ground with a bloodied face because I had already thrown a punch. Intertwined with these feelings were sorrow and regret because of the image in my ravaged mind of hurting someone who was probably a friend or I would not have been talking to him/her in the first place.

Fear of blurting out obscenities or insults

I was plagued with this symptom in countless situations for over 30 years. It struck most commonly during weddings, funerals, church services or other similar formal ceremonies.

Fear of doing something else embarrassing
    I have had so many incidents of this symptom that
the illustrations could be endless. A good example would
be fear that I might faint while speaking in public.

Fear that you will act on unwanted impulses
(e.g., to stab a loved one)
    Of all the symptoms in the AGGRESSIVE OBSES-
SIONS category, this one tormented me the most. For
instance, it was difficult for me to use tools because I
feared I would use them to attack and hurt someone.
Hammers were the most obsession-provoking item due
to the damage they could do if I ever acted upon the
impulse. My efforts to be productive at work or have
fun at play were constantly short-circuited.

Fear that you will harm others by not being
careful enough (e.g., driving over someone)
    I would pull up to a traffic signal at an intersection
or a stop sign and fear that I would floor the accelera-
tor of the car and run down people crossing the street
in front of me. During traumatizing episodes, I would
put the car in park in an effort to keep myself from
acting out the impulse. This is a very frightening symptom and difficult to talk about because, until I knew
others had had this symptom, it sounded too stupid
and embarrassing to discuss even with my doctors.

Fear that you will be responsible for a horrible
occurrence (e.g., fire or burglary)
    This fear would come into play with several of the
fears discussed earlier. In my bedeviled mind, if some
of the other fears had been acted upon, this symptom
would have followed like a chain reaction of events

unfolding. The end result for me was a supercharge of anxiety as I fought back to keep it from happening.

CONTAMINATION OBSESSIONS

Concern or disgust with bodily waste or secretions (e.g., urine, feces, saliva)
I did not have this symptom. *

Concern with dirt or germs
Among the many symptoms, this was one of the first to develop and the most difficult to defeat. At one point during my teenage years, I was so fearful of eating contaminated food that I was 30 pounds underweight. I was literally starving myself to death because I was so irrationally afraid of germs. This symptom forms the premise or is the basis for all of the symptoms listed under the category "Cleaning/Washing Compulsions" which I will discuss in detail in later in this chapter.

Excessive concern with environmental contaminants (e.g., asbestos, radiation, toxic waste)
I did not have this symptom. *

Excessive concern with household chemicals or cleaning agents
I did not have this concern. *

Excessive concern with animals, insects, etc.
I did not have this symptom. *
In fact, my fox terrier dog, Corky, was my best friend and a definite stabilizer in my turbulent childhood. He had to be put to sleep at the very old age of 18 (1954-1972). I still miss him.

Fear of sticky substances or residues
I did not have this symptom. *

Concern that you will become ill
This symptom ties in with "concern with dirt or germs" discussed earlier. Sickness was one of my major fears, to the point of undiagnosed hypochondriasis.

Concern that you will get others ill
I did not have this symptom. *

Concern with diseases (e.g., AIDS, hepatitis, etc.)
My concerns in this category were no greater than the normal person's. Apparently, I rationalized the odds of becoming ill with such diseases were much lower than everyday illness because the spread of many of these diseases is believed to be controlled by personal behavior.

TROUBLE WITH SEXUAL OBSESSIONS

Forbidden or perverse sexual thoughts,
images or impulses
Nothing beyond the normal range of feelings.

Thoughts or impulses involving
children or incest
I did not have this symptom. *

Inappropriate sexual behavior towards others
I did not have this symptom. *

TROUBLE WITH HOARDING/SAVING OBSESSIONS

Examples: magazines, papers, trash, other items

When my OCD was at its incapacitating level during my teenage years, this symptom was very intense. I saved chewing gum and candy wrappers out of fear that something unknown and awful would happen to me if I did not. I never knew what the "something" was, just that "it" would happen if I failed to obey. At least no one ever had an opportunity to call me a litterbug!

RELIGIOUS OBSESSIONS (scrupulosity)

Concern with sacrilege, blasphemy and sinfulness, excessive concern with right or wrong, morality, trouble with religious images or thoughts

None of these symptoms affected me. *

I grew up in the Presbyterian Church and served that church in several capacities, including being a ruling elder for several years. I was never troubled with anything out of the ordinary.

OBSESSIONS WITH NEED FOR SYMMETRY, EXACTNESS OR ORDER, SOMATIC OBSESSIONS

Concern with illness or disease

This symptom co-mingles with some of the contamination obsessions discussed previously. That is, after I obsessed over dirt or germs, I would begin to carry the process to the next level by worrying about what disease or other illness would be caused by those germs.

Such intense and prolonged fear about what might or could occur then leads to anxiety and panic attacks. Any muscle ache or inconsequential pain would only serve to "confirm" that my totally irrational fears were becoming reality.

Excessive concern with body parts or aspect of appearance

Nothing symptomatic or beyond the normal range of feelings.

CLEANING/WASHING COMPULSIONS

Excessive hand-washing

This is one of the most constant, low-level and ongoing symptoms in my case. It ties in with "concern with dirt and germs" and "concern with illness." By washing my hands, I was fitfully trying to prevent the fears in the other categories from coming to fruition. I never washed my hands to the point that they became red and raw as many OCD sufferers do. Rather, I washed my hands quickly between picking up things, such as putting a tool away and getting another out to use, for example. This process made usually simple tasks around the house or office take seemingly forever to perform.

Excessive showering or bathing

I did not have this symptom. *

Excessive toothbrushing, grooming or toilet routine

I did not have this symptom. *

Excessive cleaning of household items
or other objects
I did not have this symptom. *

Use of special cleaners to remove "contamination"
Nothing special...ordinary bar soap was good enough
for me!

Use of other measures to prevent
contact with or remove "contamination"
I did not have this symptom. *

CHECKING COMPULSIONS

Need to check that you did not/will not
harm others
I did not have this symptom. *

Need to check that you did not/will not harm self
This was a constant and bothersome symptom, especially during teenage and early adult years. I would
walk in patterns on carpets and tile floors and count
my steps to prevent something unknown and awful
from happening to me. If I did not do the pattern "right,"
or the step count was off, I had to go back down the hall
or come into the room a second time or whatever repeatedly until I got it right. What was "right" was a
decision made as illogically as the mechanism triggering the episode in the first place. I believe this is to
have been one of my more publicly noticeable symptoms simply because it is pretty hard not to be seen
going back and forth on a downtown sidewalk or in an
office building hallway. When I thought someone with
me or passing nearby was aware of my "difficulty," I

would fake looking for a dropped pen or coins or look toward the sky if a plane was passing overhead, but I would really be counting my steps or thinking my patterns furiously.

Need to check that nothing terrible did/will happen and need to check that I did not make a mistake
These symptoms were co-mingled with the one just discussed above.

Need to check because of somatic obsessions (e.g., check body parts)
I did not have this symptom. *

REPEATING RITUALS

Need to reread or rewrite
I had both of them. They made studying in school and working extremely difficult for me. I would add a third one: retracing my writing. At one time, it was nearly impossible for me to write a check because of this element.

Need to repeat activities (e.g., crossing threshholds, going in/out door, up/down from chair, tying shoes, dressing/undressing
Sadly, you name it and I have done it under this heading. The variations are never-ending. It dominated my days as a teenager. At one time, it took me until noon each day to get dressed. After a normal shower, I would spend four to five hours putting my clothes on and then taking them off — repeating the process almost endlessly. Anxiety and panic attacks were ram-

pant. At the end of each episode, I was exhausted and felt weak and tired. I needed some four or five hours to undress at bedtime as I literally reversed the process. All day long, I repeated routine activities in endless succession. I was a slave. I rarely achieved anything productive during this era. Reading this may seem comical and unbelievable to the unenlightened, but it is very sad for me to think about. All that school time and playtime lost...forever. The only irreplaceable commodity in life is time. This was a helluva a way for a physically healthy, good looking young guy with a genius I.Q. to have spent several valuable years of his life!

COUNTING COMPULSIONS
ORDERING/ARRANGING COMPULSIONS
HOARDING/COLLECTING COMPULSIONS
MISCELLANEOUS OBSESSIONS

Need to know or remember

When I was riding in a car, I used to repeat and try to remember license tag numbers on passing vehicles. I would be silently repeating them over and over as I saw them. Busy streets and heavy traffic put me in a real bind because I could not keep up with the high volume. The solution was to stay home during morning and afternoon rush hours when the traffic was heavy. Also, I used to copy the serial numbers off of paper money before spending it for purchases. If I did not obey these obsessions, surely something unknown and awful would happen to me as punishment. In other words, I constantly felt fearful and threatened.

Fear of saying certain things

This symptom functions in tandem with "fear of blurting out obscenities or insults" which was discussed earlier.

Fear of saying just the right thing

Yes, I had this symptom, but I don't know what to say about it now! That's what improvement or recovery is like!

Trouble with intrusive images

The intrusive images were faces of people I either disliked or had had some recent conflict with over any kind of issue. I could break up these images by "overpowering" them with thoughts of either my parents, the high school head football coach, the Presbyterian minister, my psychiatrist or certain "special" fraternity brothers. Let me explain. Frequently, I would obsess over people I had been in recent conflict with and end up in a full-blown anxiety attack. The individual's face as it appeared during the negative interaction would become frozen in my mind's eye and destroy my ability to move on or think about anything else. The only way I could break up these episodes would be by battling to get the image of some "safe" person in my mind's eye. After a period of minutes, which often seemed much longer, the "safe" figure would drown out or overpower the "unsafe" image. As this occurred, the intense anxiety symptoms would subside almost immediately. While the "mental fireworks" were going on between these "safe/unsafe" figures, it was impossible for me to do anything else. If I was distracted in the middle of one of these sieges by a telephone call, for example, I would answer it and probably come across to the caller as inattentive, disinterested or otherwise distracted. At the end of the call, the siege resumed with its previous intensity until the overpowering mechanism could defeat it. It was as if a boxing match were going on inside my head. My thoughts were as scrambled as when a bowling ball hits all ten pins on a perfect strike.

Trouble with intrusive nonsense sounds, words or music
I did not have this symptom. *

Bothered by sounds/noises
I did not have this symptom. *

Fear of making mistakes
I did not have this symptom. *

Concern with certain colors
I did not have this symptom. *

Superstitious fears
This is also known as "magic thinking" among psychologists and psychiatrists. This symptom was one of the longest running and the most intense in my case. There are the more mundane ones, like not crossing the path of a black cat, to the more irrational such as turning a light switch on and off a certain number of times until it was "OK" to leave in one position, stepping over cracks in a sidewalk very gingerly or walking only on certain blocks of a linoleum tile floor. If I failed to obey or violated one of these "orders," in my mind there would be retribution to pay. I did not know what it would be, when it would come or how it might

manifest itself, but it WOULD happen.

Concern with certain numbers

Yes, I had this one. I could count on it! My magic numbers usually were 5, 7 and 10; NEVER 13. Specifically, when I would do some of the items described under "superstitious fears," I would count them in sets of 5, 7 or 10 and then repeat the sequence over and over until I got it right. There were times when the sequential repetitions were almost endless. About the only way to break them up or end them would be the "overpowering" technique discussed earlier.

MISCELLANEOUS COMPULSIONS

Mental rituals (other than checking or counting)

There have been extended periods, particularly during teenage and early adult years, when I was almost constantly doing mentally some ritual. These episodes made concentration on almost anything else virtually impossible. This may explain why studying school subjects was so difficult for me, even outside of the confinement of a classroom.

Need to tell or confess

I did not have this symptom. *

Need to touch, tap or rub

These compulsions worked in tandem with several others and were devastating to my sense of well-being and self-esteem. A simple function, changing a light bulb, for example, could result in my tapping the light bulb countless times on the socket before screwing it in. I might use a count of 5, 7 or 10 as mentioned earlier or, in my really sick days, tap repeatedly in sets of 50 or 100 or more before making the final installation. If the object was a floor lamp with a shade or a ceiling light with a globe, the entire tapping process had to be repeated in both the removal and the replacement of the shade or globe. As nutty as it sounds to those who have never had the illness, there was a controlling force that made me go through the process endlessly. As I began to get well, I was able to "negotiate" the numbers of repetitions lower until I could do the function almost like anyone else. Such efforts could be considered self-imposed behavior modification.

Measures to prevent (not by checking): harm to self; harm to others; terrible consequences
I did not have this symptom. *

Ritualized eating behaviors
This symptom was covered under the topic, "concern with dirt or germs." The OCD victim ritualizes his/her eating as one way of assuring himself/herself that the food is "safe" to eat.

Superstitious actions
Overlaps or is very similar to "superstitious fears" described earlier.

Pulling hair (from scalp, eyebrows, eyelashes, pubic hair etc.)
I did not have this symptom. *

Acts of self-damage or self-mutilation (such as picking face or other locations on the body)
During particularly severe anxiety attacks, I would

pinch the left side of my chin with my one thumb and forefinger to the point of bleeding. At the same time, the same fingers on my other hand would pinch the flesh on my left side just above the beltline. This action would help me slow my breathing and relieve severe gaggy feelings. I frequently experienced cold sweats, shakes and trembling and dizziness during these sieges. Such episodes would hit me with little notice and no visible reason and last from a few minutes to several hours. The longer an episode lasted, the weaker and more exhausted I felt and the longer it took to recover. For several years, I cut my own hair with electric clippers because using a professional barber was a sure way to trigger a mega-episode. Anytime I felt confined (trapped or caged), these kinds of feelings would hit full-force and leave me weak and badly shaken as they subsided. Such anxiety/panic attacks began in 1956 at the age of eight.

Requests for reassurance from others

My mother and father must have almost gone nuts from my asking "will I be all right..?", "will I survive the night..?" or "why can't I be normal..?" when one of the above episodes hit me. My mother would sit up much of the night praying and quoting Bible passages to me until relief came. Sometimes, it was just a matter of waiting for the medicine to take effect; other times, I simply fell asleep from exhaustion. I remember these nights as what it must be like to be awake through a full-blown nightmare, a slow and painful kind of torture unbelieveable and unbearable in scope. Such episodes were a regular occurrence for me through college and into early adulthood. I often wondered as a small boy and a young man, "what could I have ever done to deserve this kind of punishment?" It brings back uncomfortable memories to think (or write) about these incidents.

Other troubling symptoms, not included in the above list as it appeared in the book, *When Once Is Not Enough...Help for Obsessive Compulsives*, have been clearly evident in my case.

I have had severe pervasive concentration problems. This may not be surprising in view of the nature and intensity of the symptoms described earlier. One way to illustrate the concentration problems is to compare each with a static-filled AM radio signal on a summer night. The stations closest to the radio receiver have the loudest, clearest reception. But as the listener moves the dial selector off of the strong or close-in signals (stations), it becomes much more difficult to hear the weaker, more distant signals as the selector is moved across the frequencies on the AM band. On a hot, humid summer night, lightning, heat refractions and other seasonal atmospheric conditions can make all but the strongest AM stations unlistenable. Hopefully, this explains my concentration problems in an understandable way to those who have not had the experience. My concentration or train of thought was constantly being interrupted or short-circuited by my affliction.

Slowness or a delayed response in general functioning is a problem for many OCD sufferers. In the book, *When Once Is Not Enough,* the authors state, "This may be the result of having to do many rituals in the course of ordinary activities, or may represent a type of compulsive behavior itself. For example, a person may become so meticulous in doing ordinary things like eating or dressing "just right" that these activities take hours and allow little time for anything else during the day."

The last symptom is a low energy level. The tired, generally "drained" feeling may emanate from depression associated with OCD/Anxiety Disorder.

I have listed all of the generally accepted symptoms of OCD. Please keep in mind that no two OCD patients will experience exactly the same symptoms or combination of symptoms. For more information, the reader may check the OCD references listed in the back of this book or contact the city or county public mental health center nearest you for specific diagnostic information.

4

What Did I Learn from My Father?

Triumph did follow adversity, but it took years of lonely, dogged determination to find a measure of success and feeling of normalcy. There were still many jolting chuckholes, psychologically speaking, along the road. After resuming my education under heavy medication (20 milligrams of Valium and four teaspoonfuls of Elixir Alurate per day) on a part-time schedule my sophomore year in high school, my senior year turned into a nightmare of grief and sorrow.

On November 7, 1965, my father announced that he would permanently close his full-line downtown men's clothing store after 38 years in business. Joe Vaughan Men's Clothing offered its customers the best of quality and image with then-prestigious names like Hart, Schaffner & Marx, Joseph & Feiss, Bostonian Shoes and Dobbs Hats. It was first class.

It was his intention to devote full time to a savings and loan association where he had already been president for many years. Retailing had changed dramatically in the 1960s as chain stores took over more and more of the marketplace from independents and downtowns declined across the country as retail centers with the emergence of suburban enclosed malls and strip shopping centers. Crime, a lack of parking, decaying infrastructure and other urban problems hastened the demise of central business districts as retail centers.

Kansas City, Kansas, an aging, blue-collar industrial town in the Midwest, was no exception. Crime ultimately became the compelling reason to close the store. The summer of 1965 brought the Watts riot in Los Angeles. I remember my dad saying a similar situation could occur in Kansas City, Kansas. In July, 1964, dozens of police were called in to quell an all-night disturbance in a minority business district about a mile from the downtown area. My father observed that rioters could not do too much to a bank or an office building, but they would be able to carry off a clothing store in a few minutes. After the deadly Watts melee the following year, he actually talked about and contemplated purchasing guns and then he, my Uncle Fred, the store manager and I would sleep inside the building and attempt to protect it if disturbances broke out. Fortunately, the summer of 1965 passed without incident in Kansas City, Kansas.

Had the clothing store been directly affected by crime?

Well, in the last five years it was open, there were eight burglaries or attempted break-ins, five of which were successful. Our financial losses had been so great that Lloyd's of London, the insurer of last resort, became our only source of insurance coverage. Street crimes of various types, including purse snatchings, shoplifting, car break-ins and vandalism, had become pervasive in downtown Kansas City, Kansas, by the early '60s.

After one of the break-ins, investigation revealed

that the stolen merchandise was being fenced by the crooks a short distance from the store. The thieves stripped the store and brand labels off of each garment and then sold the stolen property. The burglars could not be brought to justice because one of the police detectives working the case was later determined to be involved with the burglars.

One of the keys to recovery for me, in the early stages, was working for my father at the store. I waited on customers in each department which allowed me to build up my self-confidence and have contact with people. Selling on the floor allowed me to have the freedom to move around and did not present the scary and insurmountable challenge that sitting in the tightly-packed classrooms thrust upon me. I also ran deliveries, worked in shipping and receiving, performed a variety of janitorial duties and helped decorate or trim five huge display windows which faced the street. Wrestling a shirt, tie, jacket and slacks on and off of the mannequins was a hassle, but was also a productive experience. I could do it by myself, find contentment and feel like I was accomplishing something. I started in 1963 at 75 cents an hour.

What is most important, I had an unusual opportunity to get to know my father and participate in his world which few teenagers ever get. I have realized the significance of this more and more with the passage of time because he died when I was only 18 years old. Seeing how he functioned at work and as a prominent civic leader, in addition to seeing him at home, provided me with a deeper, more mature and insightful relationship that many sons never have or only get through the passage of time which was not an option for me because of his premature death. I was able to

observe and pick up his values and ethics in the work-
place, the community and at home. He was unusually
adept at relating to people of many different socioeco-
nomic, racial and ethnic backgrounds in a city known
for its multicultural makeup and diversity. He was a
moderate who frequently used the word "fair" or fair-
ness in discussing local issues.

What I saw was a man doing more than running one
of the city's most successful retail stores. By watching
and listening, I saw him live the values and ethics he
had learned from his father as a teenager squirting
sodas behind the fountain in my grandfather's drug
store. That is, with power and position in a community
come the responsibility to give back and that each person is important, regardless of his station in life. He
was the middle child of five children whose mother died
in childbirth when he was 11.

One of the most profound examples of my father's
early influence on my long-term thinking and development was reflected in a simple incident that happened
with my daughter, Lauren Elizabeth, when she was
five years old. One evening after dinner, we were scan-
ning the TV channels to see what was on. As we passed
one channel, three black women were on stage, holding microphones and singing. Lauren asked: "Daddy,
why are black people always singing?" Like a flashback,
I recalled an answer to a similar question my father
gave to me when I was about eight or nine years old.
He had said: "Because throughout much of their history, their religion and music were all they had to hold
on to."

In the original incident with me, my father had
picked me up after Sunday School on a Sunday morning. He was on the school board and said that he wanted

to go look at a school building where an addition was under construction.

I remember it like it was yesterday. We drove down a street enroute to the school just as two black churches across the street from each other were dismissing members following services. Cars and people crowded the narrow residential street. I believe this occurred about the time former President Dwight D. Eisenhower sent federal troops into Little Rock, Arkansas, in 1957 to enforce an integration order at Little Rock's Central High School.

As we passed the churchgoers, I asked: "Daddy, if Negroes (1950s terminology) are so bad, why are they in church on Sunday morning?" My father's response was clear and instructive: "Because throughout their history in America, their religion has been all they've had to hold on to."

It was deja vu when my daughter asked me a similar question three decades later. I had not thought of that Sunday morning so long ago until my daughter unexpectedly popped her question to me. Then I responded to her like my Dad had responded to me, modifying the statement only by saying "blacks" instead of "Negroes" and by adding the reference to music.

These stories about my father are not dramatic, but, collectively, they define and illustrate his integrity and concern for others. One philosophical phrase he repeated to me many times about helping the less fortunate stated very clearly: "There but by the grace of God go I." Enough said.

My only grandparent (maternal grandmother, Ethel S. "Dee Dee" Wilkinson) died just 12 days before Christmas in 1965. She was a month short of her 89th birthday and had declined sharply in the year before her death from pneumonia and old-age complications. She had been a source of love and support and a refuge of sorts for me.

More devastating and painful setbacks lay just ahead. In the spring of 1966, just two months after ending his close-out sale, my father began having severe back pains. Initially, he was hospitalized and put in traction for a slipped disc. But that was neither the problem nor the cure. On May 18th, he underwent back surgery at another hospital. The diagnosis: terminal cancer of the kidney. He died August 27, 1966.

I was NOT told he had cancer and was dying until AFTER he was dead! The intensity of my own affliction blinded me from what I later realized was obvious as he lay in a hospital bed heavily drugged month after month. I had no last visits, father-son talks or a chance to say thanks or good-bye. By the time I was fully aware of how the situation had been handled, some 15 years later, all the doctors involved in his case had died and were unavailable to answer my many lingering questions. My mother maintains steadfastly to this day that she had not been informed of his terminal condition, did not believe he was dying and was only told of the cause of death posthumously.

My Aunt Georgia Vaughan (widow of my father's older brother, Charles) unraveled the unresolved mystery for me — 25 years later. My mother spent six weeks in the hospital in the spring of 1991. I called my Aunt Georgia one afternoon to update her on my mother's recovery from major surgery. She asked me if I had a few minutes because there was something she thought I should know. She then revealed that my mother knew my father had been diagnosed with terminal cancer BEFORE the May 18, 1966, surgery. Aunt Georgia said that she did not know why my mother "protected" me from reality, but she felt someone had to tell me the truth sometime. I did not know and decided not to ask the elderly woman why she had withheld the information for so long or made the decision to tell me that particular afternoon. We had been in regular contact over the years so estrangement was not a factor in her holding back.

I have never said anything to my mother about Aunt Georgia's unexpected revelations. After 25 years, there would be no purpose served in confronting her over the matter. Besides, the relationship between my mother and Aunt Georgia would be destroyed if I broached the subject of my father's death and told her what my Aunt had said. Whatever my mother's reasoning, I was convinced it had come from twisted thinking and NOT any evil intent to deceive me. I will be forever grateful to Aunt Georgia.

Like the venerable turtle, I made slow, but steady progress in every aspect of my life during the next two years while earning a two-year Associate of Arts degree from Kansas City Kansas Community College. My expanding capabilities and activities included a regular classroom schedule; advancement as a writer/ reporter on the staff of the student newspaper, *The Jayhawk*; being the PA announcer at home basketball games and working in my mother's successful county-wide political campaign for a seat on the newly created community college board of trustees.

In the community, I became active with De Molay, a young men's Masonic group sponsored by the Masons and I took the lead in setting up a student government day in City Hall with then Kansas City, Kansas, Mayor Joseph H. McDowell, a close family friend and another of my heroes and role models as a young adult in the years just after my father's death. In his book, *Building A City, A Detailed History of Kansas City, Kansas*, the lawyer and former state senator credited my grandfather, the late W. Lee Vaughan, Sr., with being one of the most influential people in his youth. He said my grandfather's talk about civic affairs and community responsibilities focused him toward a career in law and public service.

My overall progress was further demonstrated by my socializing more with men and dating occasionally. I resumed playing golf at Victory Hills Country Club. The level of medication remained unchanged from what was administered in high school and I continued to see Dr. O'Hearne four or five times a month for one-hour visits in his office.

5

Leaving Home and
Entering a Man's World

The fall of 1968 marked the next and, so far, most significant turning point in my growth and development. Not only did I make a successful transition to the large (18,000 enrollment) and intimidating University of Kansas campus in Lawrence, but I moved into the Sigma Alpha Epsilon Fraternity House as a member of the fall pledge class. This was the first time I had ever tried to live away from home and, as an only child, the first time I had ever had to live with and assimilate into a group.

A strange, inspiring kind of magic enveloped me when I moved into that beat-up, old frat house, surrounded by 90-some other high-energy young guys. My father and two of his brothers had lived in that same house as college men and that was a compelling motivation in my magnetic desire to be a part of that place. It had been just two years since my father's deadly bout with cancer and, in my quiet, private time late at night ("study hours" as they were known), I thought of him frequently and wondered if he or my uncles had ever lived, studied, slept or participated in other "brotherly activities" in the room where I was at that moment. I wondered what frat life, the campus, and soci-

ety in general might have been like when they were
there in the late '20s and early '30s.

It was not an obsessive or ghostly experience, but
quite the opposite, peaceful, reassuring and comfort-
ing, almost as if his spirit were there or some sort of
abstract transcendental communication were occurring
that gave me strength, power and energy I had never
experienced before and have not since.

All through my childhood, my dad had talked about
the fraternity and what it had meant to him while he
was a student at the University of Kansas School of
Law. When we went to Saturday afternoon football
games, we often stopped by the frat house to see friends
and renew old acquaintances. I was intrigued with the
hope of some day living there. In retrospect, I believe
the deep, lifetime relationship he had with SAE formed
the foundation for the almost-supernatural feelings and
experiences I have just described in my attempt to live
away from home after my shadowy existence in junior
and senior high school. My fraternity brothers became
my surrogate family. And I had proved I could live in a
man's world.

My first roommate match up seemed to be like di-
vine destiny. He had grown up in Arkansas City, Kansas, about 15 miles southeast of Wichita, and was also
a junior pledge interested in broadcast journalism. Like
me, he was also an only child, a Presbyterian and a
Senior De Molay. He and I had several classes together,
occasionally double dated or hit the bars together
around Lawrence and generally palled around. We even
did our laundry together at a nearby laundromat. Although I may have exhibited some eccentric or border-
line behavior from time to time, he never knew the
travail and agony I experienced almost constantly. If

he was aware that I was a bit odd or had "special" problems (he was a doctor's son), he never let on or said anything. He seemed to accept me as he found me and I was thankful for that and comfortable with him as a fraternity brother, friend and roomy.

I became involved on campus as well as in the classroom and the fraternity. My first semester, I started doing newscasts and covering stories on the university's carrier-current training station, KUOK-AM 630. I ran for the KU Student Senate from the School of Journalism during my second semester and finished fourth in a field of six candidates vying for three seats. I worked hard, got around and met a lot of students and faculty and received great personal satisfaction from the effort. Four more votes were all I had needed to win.

I voluntarily took on responsibilities for the fraternity's dishwasher/houseboy. He was a mentally retarded man in his late 20s who had been trained at a state institution to live on his own and earn a living doing domestic work. He needed a lot of help managing his personal affairs and in dealing with his landlady. It took considerable time and patience, but no one else among the 90 guys in the house was willing to devote the time to actually help the guy and not just tease and harass him and otherwise create more problems than were being solved in his already-difficult life. One of the meanest tricks I have ever seen occurred one afternoon when some guys coerced him into picking up a block of dry ice bare-handed. He did not have the capability to understand or know the danger and suffered serious burns on his hands. He was in bandages and unable to work for many days. My own affliction gave me a feeling of kinship with this man. I hated to see him taken advantage of.

The Vietnam War protests reached a fiery crescendo
at the University of Kansas on April 20, 1970. That
night, someone torched the Student Union Building,
touching off a fire that resulted in more than a million
dollars in damage (at 1970 construction costs). Fire
investigators determined that a person or persons had
put an incendiary device near an elevator shaft. The
elevator shaft had the effect of a smokestack and drew
the flames up through the five-story structure very
quickly. Incredibly, no one was hurt. No arrests were
ever made in the case. I was up and on duty for nearly
24 hours covering the story for KUOK-AM. The Radio-
Television-Film Department of the School of Journalism gave me it's "Special Performance Award" for the
coverage of the fire and for a difficult and tense series
of call-in talk show interviews I did on KUOK-AM with
representatives of the Black Student Union, which
helped ease racial tensions at the height of the campus
protests.

I was named news editor and afternoon news anchor on the University's big 100,000 watt NPR station,
KANU-FM 91.5, the following semester.

It was several years later before I realized fully the
significance that successful first year (1968-69) at KU
would have in laying the foundation for my entire future. Mastering the academically-tough and social-com-
petitive environment at the University of Kansas was
difficult, but with much courage, a lot of prayer, good
luck and supervised medication, I made it!!

I graduated with a BS degree in broadcast journalism with a minor in political science in May, 1971.

Let me explain why the period between 1968 and
1971 was such a watershed for me for the benefit of the
unenlightened and to encourage those who now suffer

from OCD and/or Anxiety Disorder. Behind the medicine and the mask of an outwardly friendly college kid was a young man filled with many fears of many things. Some were real and normal for that age group, but in my case, too many of them were irrational and, therefore, out of the range of normalcy. Everyday was like walking through an emotional minefield as I adjusted to a new and uncertain series of challenges. I could not openly expose my "ridiculous" feelings and fears to anyone. To do so would have meant instant and total rejection by professors, classmates and pledge and active fraternity brothers and led to a permanent and devastating defeat in my hope of one day having a "normal" life. For every day I survived, it became a "microscopic" bit easier to feel comfortable. The progress was slow, but constant and measurable. I was able to lower my guard and remove my mask enough to be "one of the boys" a little more on the campus and around the frat house. As the days crawled by, my comfort level increased. Correspondingly, my success in the classroom and the fraternity expanded and flourished.

The late Samuel Johnson once wrote something appropriate to me at this juncture in my life: "If a man does not make new acquaintances as he advances through life, he will soon find himself left alone. A man, sir, should keep his friendships in constant repair."

6

The Uphill Struggle to Reach a Level Playing Field: a Career Begins

My love affair with radio has been life-long. It intrigued me as a child and helped me get well as a teenager. And it would be my career as an adult.

While covering Vietnam War protests at the University of Kansas, I discovered that I had a unique and special ability to paint a word picture in the mirror of the mind. Newspapers and television lay out the news, or the event being covered, in literal terms. With radio, it is up to the newscaster to not only supply the verbal copy in describing what is happening, but the word picture as well, and do it in 40 seconds or less. Few people have or can develop that talent. I would spend hours scripting "imaginary" newscasts and then recording my voice reading the copy onto a tape recorder. Then I would play the tape back and criticize myself.

There were several well-known network journalists whose careers had a significant influence on my thinking and development during my formative years at the KU School of Journalism. Writing scripts (newscasts) for the electronic media is very different than the kind of prose necessary for print journalism. Broadcasting

requires short sentences and concise and familiar word-
ing or what's referred to as "tightly scripted" material.
The message must be clear the first time it's broadcast
because that is the only chance a listener will get to
understand the material. With a magazine or newspaper, the reader can go over the material as many times
as necessary to absorb the message. But the broadcaster gets one shot at being understood and must be
very precise or the message is lost forever.

Several KU professors cited David Brinkley, then a
member of NBC's famed "Huntley-Brinkley Report"
and now known for his "This Week With David
Brinkley" on ABC, and ABC Radio's legendary Paul
Harvey as good role models for learning broadcast news
writing.

I had my own favorite! The late Harry Reasoner
caught my interest and attention for a variety of reasons. When I was in school, Reasoner had just left CBS'
"60 Minutes" to be teamed with the venerable Howard
K. Smith on ABC's "Evening News" program. In 1976,
Reasoner became part of network television's first male-
female anchor team when Smith retired and Barbara
Walters came over from NBC. The venture was a ratings disaster largely because of bad chemistry between
Reasoner and Walters. Two years later, Harry went
back to CBS and rejoined the "60 Minutes" program.

Reasoner's writing style was elegant, but clear of
thought and, therefore, understandable. Unlike many
contemporary broadcast journalists in this era of "ad-
vocacy journalism," Reasoner showed feeling and sen-
sitivity, but never allowed his personal opinion to become part of his reporting. His strength of character
and wisdom in pressure situations were something I
appreciated even more with the passage of time in a

business where substance and staying power seem to be professional liabilities.

The Iowa-born Reasoner had an undeniable Midwestern nasal sound in his air delivery which was his most endearing trait to me. I figured that if Harry could make it being himself at the network, maybe, just maybe if I worked hard, I could make it in Kansas City!

Because of its natural intimacy and deep, personal meaning to me in my years of personal crisis, I was always mindful of my audience. During every broadcast, I did my best to visualize who might be listening and what their situation might be at that particular moment. A professional talks TO his audience; not AT the listener. That's the difference between just being a voice in a box and really communicating the message one-to-one.

As a preschooler, I did "pretend" newscasts and weather reports while playing on my swing in the backyard. The seeds of interest may have been unwittingly planted by my dad, who, because of his interest and involvement in community affairs and politics, turned on the radio first thing every morning.

Alex Drier and Lloyd Burlington were the morning anchor voices of NBC Radio News in the 1950s. WDAF Radio's Bob Higby followed with the metro report. Until a federal antitrust lawsuit during the Eisenhower Administration divorced virtually all newspapers from radio and television stations in 1957, WDAF Radio and TV had been properties of *The Kansas City Star*, which gave the stations the advantage of *The Star's* vast resources for news coverage in that era. Significantly, it was the first NBC Radio affiliate west of the Mississippi River.

Radio played an important role in my struggle with OCD because I would set goals to have certain obsessions and rituals completed BEFORE certain daily programs came on the air. By necessity, radio is very structured. Everything that happens on a station is scheduled and timed to occur in a specific sequence. It is what's called a format. And the engineer/operator follows a "program pie" to shape that format each hour on the air. The items broadcast are then checked off on an FCC "program log" as legal verification that they were actually aired.

I became familiar with what would be scheduled to be on the air at a certain time and then attempted to have a specific ritual completed before the commercial, newscast, weather forecast, or whatever, was broadcast. It was a primitive form of self-imposed behavior therapy...and it worked! As I progressed, the awful, feared "IT" would happen to me if I did not get certain things done by a certain time. In other words, the threat or fear developed if I DID NOT have a ritual done by a specified time instead of acting on the compulsion to endlessly stretch obsessions out over long minutes or hours of time.

I was unlucky, then lucky in my first position after graduating from Kansas University. On May 10, 1971, I began working as a city hall reporter and afternoon newscaster at KEWI-AM, a 5,000 watt rock station in Topeka, the capital of Kansas. I moved into a small, cramped one-bedroom apartment with a fraternity brother who had just taken a job as a salesman at a Topeka television station.

Initially, my OCD/Anxiety symptoms were very intense and I required additional medication to function. I also had frequent bouts of stomachaches and diarrhea. What happened on July 12, 1971, was too crazy, even for the broadcast industry, but was a sign of things to come. The news director abruptly fired me one morning when I came back to the station from my morning-beat run to Topeka City Hall! He told me, without being specific, that "things were just not working out" for me in the two-man news department.

The only odd thing that had frustrated me considerably concerned reports I radioed into the station from the field on the two-way. They were not being used on the air. This had the effect of making me look unproductive while out on the street.

I requested and was granted a meeting with the general manager of the radio station. I explained that situation to him and asked for other factors involved in my getting two weeks notice. He listened and was cordial, but gave no indication of what he might be thinking during the visit.

Eleven days after he had dismissed me, the general manager fired the man who had fired me and then re-hired me as news director.

I stayed at KEWI until October 27, 1971, when I resigned to become morning news anchor and state-house reporter at WREN-AM, a legendary, tradition-rich station with a five-person news department. I was scheduled to cover the upcoming 1972 session of the Kansas Legislature for the station, which had a 5,000 watt regional signal and a strong image in the market.

WREN was owned by former Kansas Governor and 1936 Republican presidential nominee Alf M. Landon. Although then 84 years old, Landon was in the station every day and definitely was the boss. The News Director, Roy Vernon, had been there 14 years and liked me both personally and professionally. I had interviewed with him numerous times while in school, but he never had a position available to hire me.

My adjustment went very well in the new position. I was as comfortable as could be expected and getting good feedback about all phases of my work.

One of the most fascinating experiences I have ever had came in February, 1972. That was when former President Richard M. Nixon made his historic breakthrough trip to Red China. Governor, as Landon was called around the station, wanted to know everything about the Presidential trip to Peking. Several times each morning, Landon ambled down from his office to the news wire room to see what the Associated Press and the ABC Radio network were reporting on the China trip. He had the enthusiasm and effusiveness of a young colt romping across a sunbathed meadow in the spring breeze. He would emerge from the wire room ready to talk to anyone around about the latest developments.

Almost daily, I drove the Governor the short distance to a Downtown Topeka businessmen's club where he lunched and played cards each day with other icons of business and politics in the capital city. He admonished me to save all of the AP wire copy relating to the Nixon China trip and bring it with me when I picked him up in two hours. He was always ready to go when I came back. As I drove, he slowly unwound the rolled up wire copy, dragged on a cigarette he had bummed from one of his buddies and ad-libbed reaction all the way back to the station.

What a cherished experience for a then 24 year-old newsman to have had with one of the few men ever alive at any particular time in history who had been nominated by a major party for the presidency!

Alf Landon had advocated United States' recognition of Red China since shortly after the communists took control of the mainland in 1949. This stand, particularly during the intense, domestic anticommunist witch-hunt days of Wisconsin Senator Joseph McCarthy in the 1950s and early 1960s, had pushed Landon to the far left, not only of the Republican Party, but of the political spectrum of the era in general.

So, the "old man," a common and affectionate reference, clearly had a deep, personal interest in the outcome of President Nixon's journey. It was obvious that the conservative Nixon's successful trip to the ancient land of mystery and intrigue gave the liberal old political warrior a good measure of vindication after his many years of ideological isolation for advocating diplomatic recognition of the world's most populated country.

Significantly, local, regional and national news organizations called WREN Radio at regular intervals to get Landon's reaction to the political drama unfolding in Peking. His labored, methodical Midwestern style of speaking changed little through the years. Old timers said the Governor still sounded at 84 virtually the same as the man who lost every state except Maine and Vermont to Democrat Franklin D. Roosevelt in 1936.

He clearly reveled in the brief return to center stage, which included regular calls to and from the Nixon White House and to members of the Kansas Congressional delegation. After decades of being ignored as the GOP's all-time biggest loser, Landon was invited to address the Republican National Convention in August, 1972.

The joy and contentment of February came to a sudden and jolting end at the close of the legislative ses-

sion in March. Roy Vernon resigned as News Director
to become Topeka City Clerk. Roy spent a lot of time
with me after his resignation because he could see I
was shaken. He told me he was going to recommend
me to be his successor and had been going to recommend me for promotion to assistant news director if he
had not decided to take the city clerk's job.

I applied for Vernon's position and he did recommend me, but I was not selected. A previous WREN
News employee, who had been working at a radio station in Nebraska, was hired. He and the general manager had been pals during his previous tenure. He
clearly wanted to develop his own news staff and had
been given authority to do so. On Good Friday, March
30, 1972, I was fired when I arrived for work.

Ironically, he lasted less than a year as news director before resigning to return to his roots as a farmer
in southwest Iowa. I don't know how that decision was
made. I do know that running a newsroom for Alf
Landon involved plenty of pressure and responsibility. I still believe I could have done well in that spot.

7

Keeping My Nose to the Grindstone While Trying to Keep from Getting It Knocked Off

I decided to go for a real challenge and try to get into major market radio news...and I made it! I moved from Topeka to Kansas City, Kansas, and went to work July 27, 1972, as a general assignment reporter/news anchor for KCKN AM & FM, a country music station with a well-established and respected news department. The station, which simulcast the news on both AM and FM, consistently was among the top four in Arbitron audience ratings in the metro Kansas City market in the early 1970s.

KCKN Radio, once a property of *The Kansas City Kansan* daily newspaper, was in a unique situation because Kansas City, Kansas, was believed to be the largest urban-central city (1970 U.S. Census: 168,213) in the nation without a television station.

During my student days at the University of Kansas, I had been a "stringer" on campus for KCKN, covering the Vietnam War protests and doing some investigative reporting associated with those protests and frequent incidents of antiwar confrontations and violence between police and demonstrators in Lawrence. A "stringer" is a reporter in either print or electronic journalism who works on a free-lance basis and is paid a prearranged fee for each report or story turned in and actually used.

The opportunity to be a stringer provided me with valuable experience in covering hard news and getting priceless exposure on a major market outlet. As I neared graduation from KU, program director, Ted Cramer, praised my effort, but told me I needed to get some "seasoning" in a smaller market before I could join the news staff at KCKN Radio. Ted and I worked in three different radio stations under separate ownerships during my career. It is testimony to both my talent and hard work that I did not have to go to a market smaller than Topeka and was hired by KCKN Radio approximately 14 months later.

My job included filling in on the air as an anchor at various times as needed, covering city councils in the two Kansas City's, gathering information, taping interviews by telephone and writing news copy.

I had many anxiety attacks, particularly the gaggy, short-breathed feeling and other uncomfortable moments because of my OCD while working at KCKN, but my personal and professional progress was on the positive side on balance. Some people like to refer to the "good old days" when talking about a memorable past experience. I do not believe they exist. In my opinion, the "good old days" are wherever you are now, doing whatever you may be doing. However, if they did exist and I could go back to them, I wish I could go back to KCKN Radio.

One of the stories I covered concerned a new economic development program being put together by the Kansas City Kansas Area Chamber of Commerce and the Board of Public Utilities, the municipally-owned water and light utility. The program was to be funded by a $250,000 annual grant from the utility to the chamber.

I resigned from the KCKN news staff and, on May 19, 1974, I began working for this new economic development program as a public relations specialist.

In the allegedly nonpartisan 1975 city election, the economic development program became the center of controversy in the BPU incumbent board members' reelection bid. The program had been a political football between various factions in the city from its inception. There had been several lawsuits filed in District Court by representatives of both sides. The challengers claimed the BPU's contract for economic development with the chamber was an "illegal gift of public money to a private corporation." Chamber supporters countered that "the agreement was for a service to be performed, the same way the utility would contract for any other kind of service to be provided." Further, BPU, chamber and city officials claimed that, without new economic development, residential and commercial utility rates and property taxes would increase sharply. Internal bickering clouded the issue even more. The first director of the program resigned under fire following a swirl of allegations and innuendoes surrounding his performance. The situation was so unstable that his successor lived in a motel during his entire eight-month tenure.

The three incumbents up for reelection on the five-member board barely survived the February primary balloting. The writing was on the wall, as the saying goes, and the five people employed in the chamber's economic development department knew it was time to update their resumes and start looking for new jobs.

I had a sobering personal experience during the cam-

paign run-off. Because of my family background and
my visibility in radio, I became a high profile figure on
the chamber's staff. About midway through this phase
of the campaign, a prominent businessman and chamber member took me aside and warned me in terse
tones that "people who became too popular too fast can
easily be removed from the scene permanently." And
then he added threateningly, "Accidents do happen,
you know." I can still hear his curt, chilling words and
see his cold, steely glare in my mind's eye as I think
about that experience. A few days later, a political ally
of this man's reinforced the earlier "warning" while I
was in his office.

I considered filing a complaint with the Kansas City,
Kansas, Police Department, but remembered the grim
and disheartening experiences my father had had with
his many burglary investigations a decade earlier and
decided not to. In one incident, a detective on the case
was determined to be involved with the criminal fenc-
ing operation selling the stolen merchandise. The
investigation stalled and the detective was never
touched as the entire matter disappeared into the city
hall labyrinth. I was further influenced by the fact that
the federal government had launched an investigation
of the controversial department after allegations involving prostitution, vice activities and other alleged
corruption.

All of this had an unnerving effect on a young guy
(26 years old) who had taken a job to make a living and
was enthusiastic about prospects for rejuvenating his
hometown's sagging fortunes. Clearly, some people
hoping to gain control of whatever was left of the chamber after the election wanted me out of the way. The
economic development personnel accounted for half of

the staff and about one-half of the operating budget. What was left was strictly a bare-bones operation.

A chamber of commerce is not usually as politically predatory as a city hall. But then, Kansas City, Kansas, is a tough town whose bare-knuckle, back-alley politics knows neither shame nor honor. Historically, it has been considered one of the most machine-controlled cities in the country between Chicago and San Francisco.

If I had been older and more mature, I would have handled that situation very differently and would not have been so intimidated. I had the connections and the clout to call the bluff, but with my OCD/Anxiety symptoms particularly troublesome in this period, I lacked the self-confidence to marshal my forces. In retrospect, it might not have been worth it to try to continue existing in that pit-bull kind of environment.

The April, 1975, general election saw utility board members go down to defeat. The newly elected board members took office soon after and cancelled the economic development contract with the chamber of commerce on 60-days notice. My hopes that Kansas City Kansans were ready to trade the town's tattered image of topless dens of iniquity for legitimate, job-producing economic development were dashed.

Paradoxically, while my job and the people who controlled its funding were going into the tank, my mother not only led the ticket, but scored her biggest margin of victory ever in her bid for a third, four-year term on the Kansas City Kansas Community College Board of Trustees. She had led in the primary and general election balloting in the 1967 and 1971 elections and 1975 continued the string of political successes.

My search for new employment indicated that I had

survived the political firestorm at the chamber with
my credibility and integrity intact in spite of the emo-
tionally-searing experiences of the previous few
months.

On April 30, 1975, a very close associate of U.S. Senator Bob Dole of Kansas offered me a job working for the
Senator in his field office in Kansas City, Kansas. As
proposed at a series of meetings before the job offer, I
would have run the office which was then located in a
downtown high-rise office building with a secretary and
one other person under me representing Dole at various public and private functions in the northeast Kansas area, the most populated and politically diverse
region of the Sunflower State. Dole had three other
field offices in Wichita, Topeka and Parsons. The Dole
contact was very high on my talent and abilities and
stated he believed that I would be transferred to Dole's
Washington office within a year. He told me that I had
been "approved for the position" by the Dole hierarchy
of friends and advisors, including my former employer,
Governor Alf Landon.

This was an important juncture in Dole's career as
well as mine. The Republican from Russell had just
won a tough reelection battle over a popular Democrat
Congressman in 1974 and had obvious, if not announced, ambitions to occupy the White House.

He was nominated by the Republican Party to be
President Gerald R. Ford's vice presidential running
mate in 1976. The Ford-Dole ticket lost to the Democrat ducat of Jimmy Carter and Walter Mondale in
November, 1976. Dole later sought the Republican
nomination for President, but failed to capture it in
1980 and 1988. He served as Senate Majority Leader
for two years during the Reagan Administration, fol-

lowing an easy reelection bid in 1980.

Why did Dole's people want me? I was a well-qualified and talented candidate for such a position. In addition, my family name had been a long-term, proven vote-getter in the most ethnically-oriented, heavily-Democratic city in a traditionally Republican state. The Vaughans had been registered Democrats, but totally independent from the machine and patronage system that had dominated Wyandotte County, Kansas, for decades.

My connections at every level of the community could have helped build long-term "political bridges" for Senator Dole in a county he had never won and solidified his political base following his tough 1974 victory over obstetrician and U.S. Representative Bill Roy of Topeka.

But it was not to be. I thought about it long and hard and deep down I wanted to do it. However, with my OCD/Anxiety Disorder problems in an uproar following the chamber struggle and knowing the stress that would come, working for a man with Dole's pressure-cooker drive and ambition would be virtually impossible for me. Among the symptoms: short breathed, shakiness or trembling, gaggy feeling, light-headed or dizzy spells, cold/sweaty palms, cramps and/or diarrhea, concern with dirt or germs, concern that I would become ill, overconcern with illness or disease, excessive hand washing, need to check that I did not/will not harm self (constantly checking, counting episodes); repeating rituals: need to reread or rewrite, need to repeat activities (e.g., crossing thresholds, going in/out door, up/down from chair, tying shoes, dressing/undressing); superstitious fears, concern with certain numbers, mental rituals other than checking and counting, need to touch, tap or rub objects, ritualized eating behaviors, acts of self-damage or self-mutilation (such as picking face or other isolated locations on the body), fear of embarrassing myself and requests for assurance from others. These symptoms are detailed in Chapter 3.

The position would require a lot of highway driving and flying in both small, private planes and commercial airliners, something I knew I could not deal with. Being closed in for long periods of time in a car or plane gave me symptoms of panic attacks and claustrophobia. Obviously, it would be impossible to stop the plane and get out and take a walk and almost as impractical to cope with the situation in ground transportation.

Former Missouri Senator, Thomas F. Eagleton, was forced off of the 1972 Democratic ticket as George McGovern's vice presidential running mate after it became public knowledge that he had been under psychiatric care, had been hospitalized for exhaustion and had received electric shock treatment as a part of his therapy. I feared my past might cause me painful humiliation if it were to be disclosed.

The Watergate break-in and subsequent investigation and hearings in the U.S. Senate played heavily in my decision-making process. Just one year earlier, Richard M. Nixon had become the first President ever to resign, in the wake of the Watergate scandal. No matter what one's opinion was of the issues involved, many people in my age range became disillusioned with politics in the ensuing months and years following that bizarre chapter in U.S. history. My mind was clouded with a blend of cynicism, angst and apathy.

After weeks of soul-searching and cognitive pondering of all the various factors involved, I said, "Thanks, but no thanks" to Senator Dole's representative on June 6, 1975. The reasons that I gave for turning down the position were evasive. I could not state the real reasons: my almost constant OCD/Anxiety symptoms and the factors under consideration in my decision-making process as outlined above.

I considered many fine possibilities before deciding to accept a position as a public relations assistant for United Missouri Bancshares, Inc., in Kansas City, Missouri, on June 23rd of that year. My new position would become effective on July 1. Two days later, *The Kansas City Kansan* daily newspaper carried the following news story:

"Joe H. Vaughan, Jr., has resigned from the staff of the Kansas City Kansas Area Chamber of Commerce to become public relations assistant for United Missouri Bancshares, Inc., in Kansas City, Missouri. Board Chairman, R. Crosby Kemper, made the announcement.

"Vaughan is a member of the Task Force Committee on the Amateur Athletic Union National Championships and Pan-Am Trials Swim Meet in KCK Aug. 17-20; secretary of the board of directors of Sigma Alpha Epsilon Fraternity at KU and a member of the Greater Kansas City Alumni Assn.'s board of directors; ruling elder at the First United Presbyterian Church and chairman of the Christian Education Committee; member of the civic advisory board of the KCK Salvation Army; member of the Advisory Council, Huron Chapter, Order of De Molay; member of the Downtown KCK Kiwanis Club; member of the Minority Business Opportunity Committee of the U.S. Small Business Administration; life member of the Kansas University Alumni Assn.; member of the American Industrial

Development Council; member of the Wyandotte County Historical Society; member of American MENSA, Ltd.; and a former member of the board of directors of the KCK Area Jaycees.

"He is listed in the United States Jaycees' 'Outstanding Young Men of America-1975' which was released last month. Vaughan's civic awards include being voted 'Jaycee of the Month' in his chapter in June, 1973, and February, 1975. He was a member of the KCKN news team that was selected 'number one for weekend news coverage in the state of Kansas' in 1974 by the Associated Press."

I found bank marketing and public relations to be a new, energizing experience, although I did have some temporary trepidations about the department's location on the bank's 13th floor in Room 1313! There were four people in the department, including the director, a marketing person, a secretary and me. The bank had an in-house printing service, but contracted with an outside advertising agency which members of the department supervised. Only two other banks in the market were large enough to have full-time, in-house departments.

My first six months went exceedingly well. The director gave my performance a green light with several points of constructive criticism at my preliminary review on January 2, 1976, and said he would recommend a raise for me in his report to the Personnel Department.

Senator Dole came back into the picture suddenly and unexpectedly. A different person representing the Senator contacted me and then showed up in my office at the bank on January 15th. During the course of the conversation, he heaped considerable praise on me and included a new offer for me to take the field office manager's position in Kansas City, Kansas.

The fact that a man of Bob Dole's position and stature was impressed by my resume enough to solicit my services a second time was very humbling and a great compliment to me. I thought and thought about it and the possibilities made the situation a tremendous temptation. In the interim, I had received my comprehensive review at the bank January 28th and was given several additional duties and responsibilities and a ten percent salary increase. Two of those responsibilities included editing and producing the bimonthly house organ and overseeing maintenance of the 13 bank-owned billboards around the area. The future seemed sanguine.

As I agonized over the second offer from Dole, I realized that I did not have the intense passion and emotional fiber necessary for the pugnacious, pell-mell pace public service demands. The bitter experiences at the Chamber of Commerce were etched in my mind. So, regretfully, I called the Dole contact on February second and turned down the position.

UMBI was entering a major growth period. Changes in state and federal regulations in the mid-70s had allowed United Missouri to become a multi-bank holding company with facilities in 19 cities across the state and just under a billion dollars in assets. The lead bank, United Missouri Bank of Kansas City, was the second largest bank in the metropolitan area and the 192nd largest out of more than 14,000 commercial banks in the nation.

Mr. Kemper was a "hands-on" owner/chairman and personally approved virtually every news release, advertisement, billboard or other similar projects the department was responsible for or produced. This meant I had the opportunity to be in his office several times a week on an almost unrestricted basis to obtain these approvals. His public persona is that of a gruff, tempestuous, abrasive individual, but I found him to be warm and cordial, although formal at all times. Like my father, he always spoke precisely and looked you in the eye. I quickly picked up on the approach, the style and the image he wanted his bank(s) to project, then developed that kind of material each time I made a presentation to him. I learned and grew considerably through observing his decision-making process on these questions.

He is a member of a prominent family that is well known regionally in banking, civic and social circles, but it is his physical presence that added an additional dimension when he walked into a room. His ruddy, ruggedly handsome face and booming voice topped his six-foot, seven-inch approximately 240-pound frame.

I remember one afternoon in particular when he asked me to accompany him to a luncheon where he was to be the guest speaker. All of the bank's full-size executive cars were already in use. The only car in the garage was a small Volkswagen Rabbit used for deliveries. He was not a happy man after stuffing himself into that sardine can-sized car and made no effort to hide his displeasure with the vitriolic comments he made as we went to and from the luncheon engagement. Not only did he have to remove his trademark felt hat, but his knees were at eye level in front of his face against the dashboard as we rolled down the street. We never went anywhere in that car again!

One of my biggest projects was writing a detailed history of UMB-KC, which dates back to 1913. The booklet included photographs and information about Mr. Kemper's extensive art collection as displayed throughout the building as well as information about the various departments and the many services available to both the retail and commercial banking client. Several times a month, tour groups came through the bank. Many of these people were school children on field trips, correspondent bank clients and other friends/clients of UMB-KC who wanted to see the nuts and bolts of the operation. The publication gave them something to take home and kept the bank and its services before them as a public relations/sales tool.

I also took great pride in a comprehensive metropolitan street map I produced, which was made available to customers of all the banking facilities around the area. It was designed to be kept in the customer's vehicle glove box or attache case and included several direct and indirect selling messages on each side of the map.

During this period, I was invited twice to be an escort for the debutantes of American Royal BOTAR Ball. The Belles of the American Royal (BOTAR) serve as hostesses and ambassadors and officially kick off the American Royal Livestock, Horse Show and Rodeo each fall at the end of harvest time. It is considered one of the most significant events of its kind in the nation. My father had served on the Royal's Board of Governors in the 1940s and early '50s, while my mother was the soprano at the annual Kansas Day activities for many years.

One of my proudest accomplishments was being named Chairman of the Kansas City, Kansas, Salvation Army's 1976 Christmas Fund Drive. A then-record $50,645 was contributed, exceeding the announced goal of $45,000. Numerous personal calls and telephone calls to businesses and industries were necessary to drum up support. Hundreds of civic club members were marshalled to serve as bell ringers in shopping centers with the familiar red kettles. The annual effort to help the most needy residents of the city during the Christmas holiday season had raised less than $40,000 in 1975.

Earlier that same year, I served as Publicity Chairman for Project Concern's Greater Kansas City Walk for Mankind. Over 49,000 residents of the metropolitan area pledged $133,461 to 4,686 walkers who participated. Project Concern, an international health care organization which operates in underdeveloped countries, allows a percentage of the money collected to stay in the community. In 1976, the local share went to the Burn Unit at the University of Kansas Medical Center. Leadership roles in major fund-raising efforts like these are hard work, but the successful end brings joy and an exhilarating feeling.

Rapidly emerging changes in the banking industry in general and the bank holding company's fast growth brought uncertainty and turmoil. Three department directors, three advertising agencies and two years later, my tenure at UMBI ended with my dismissal.

Medically, the years at UMBI were a period of fewer symptoms. There were extended periods where I did not use Elixir Alurate and only needed Valium occasionally. My appointments with Dr. O'Hearne were reduced to monthly visits.

Upon my departure, Mr. Kemper handed me the following letter which said, in part: "...executed his duties while at United Missouri Bank and did fine credit to himself..."

Benjamin Franklin is quoted as saying, "The only sure things in life are death and taxes." I submit that another element should be added to Franklin's timeless observation: "The only sure things in life are death, taxes AND CHANGE."

Change is inevitable and unavoidable.

8

Christine Craft Wasn't the Only Kansas City Broadcast Journalist to File a Discrimination Lawsuit in the 1980s and Win!

Accepting failure was not an option. The reverse discrimination lawsuit in the case of Vaughan vs. Taft Broadcasting (WDAF-AM in Kansas City, Mo.), was filed on the basis of principle, not color. I had been working at WDAF-AM in the news department for 33 months, nearly three years, when a psychological lightning bolt hit me on Wednesday, March 28, 1979.

As I was about to leave for the day at 12:30 p.m., News Director Charles Gray called me into his office. Instantly, I sensed by the tone of his voice on the intercom that something very bad had either happened or was about to happen. Gray asked me to come in, close the door and sit down. I instantly observed that he seemed tense and nervous. His face was flushed and he was slowly wringing his hands as his elbows rested on the arms of the chair. The stoic-looking, macho veteran newsman rarely showed emotion, but on this occasion he could barely contain it.

Seeing his appearance triggered a strong reaction in me. I felt drained and weak and began to break into a cold sweat as Gray started to talk in a shaky voice, repeatedly clearing his throat.

He spoke slowly, choosing his words carefully. Gray said that the decision had been made to fire me and that I was to empty my desk, remove all personal property from the station and return all station keys and property immediately.

I asked him why. He responded slowly, again choosing his words carefully. He said my "air sound was not acceptable," declining to be specific about what aspect of it was deemed deficient. My pulse quickened and my breathing became shallow as his words began to sink in. I could not believe it. I was angry, shocked and saddened because I knew I had not failed.

Throughout my tenure, I had been given increasing duties and responsibilities. My reviews had been good. Nothing verbally or in writing had reflected any supervisory or management dissatisfaction with my overall performance. There had been the usual criticisms and critiques from Gray on how to do certain things better or perform more efficiently, but I would have been more alarmed and taken notice if I had not been getting that kind of feedback. My relationship with Gray had been good enough that he frequently called me "buddy" when we were working together in the newsroom.

My role in the news department was to be there at 5 a.m., Monday through Friday, to back up Gray. I made telephone calls to more than two dozen law enforcement agencies, fire departments and other emergency public service agencies. I wrote stories from the information that I had gathered and regularly checked the Associated Press, United Press International, National Weather Service and metro city news wires for routine and breaking news and weather developments. I also coordinated traffic and weather information with the "Sky Spy" airborne traffic reporter.

When Gray was away for any reason, I became the on-air news anchor, responsible for two, scripted five-minute newscasts each hour between 5:55 and 8:55 a.m. Another employee was called in to fill in behind me in such situations. I also filled in for "Sky Spy" on traffic, but did not fly the single-engine, fixed-wing aircraft because I was not a licensed pilot and hiring a pilot to fly me would not have been cost effective. Therefore, I was provided with a fully-equipped news cruiser and reported traffic and road conditions on a two-way radio. The announcer referred to me as the "Ole Ground Hound Hangin' 'Round" when introducing me on the air. There were 28 "Sky Spy" traffic reports per day, 14 during the peak morning drive rush hours and 14 more during afternoon drive time. I liked to do traffic more than any other assignment at WDAF-AM Radio.

In the ensuing days following my hiring, I recalled hearing constantly around the radio station that the next person hired would have to be a minority. I had absolutely no problem with that. But it did seem odd that, the Monday morning following my dismissal, a black male newsman, who had been working at another radio station in the market, was already in my position.

My view was that, if a minority person was needed, the situation should have been handled either through attrition or by adding the person to the staff before getting so close to an FCC compliance deadline — NOT by firing an established veteran staff member who had the least tenure; thereby seriously damaging, if not destroying, his professional career.

I decided to consult a lawyer whose firm was strong in labor law. But I knew I could not tell my attorney about my OCD/Anxiety symptoms because exposing the REAL reason for my firing was the motivating factor and because it would be too overwhelming for him to understand.

The law firm researched the available information in great detail before advising me that there was considerable evidence to indicate that I had been wrongfully fired. Efforts to negotiate with Taft Broadcasting over the matter met with repeated failure.

A lawsuit was filed on April 25, 1980. To protect friends and former coworkers from possible retribution and because of prevailing libel and slander laws, news media accounts with attribution are used to explain the outcome of the trial.

The Associated Press carried the following on November 16, 1983:

"A veteran radio newsman who claimed he was fired because he was white has won a $173,000 judgement from a Jackson County jury.

"Joe Vaughan, 35, who now is news director at KLWN-AM/KLZR-FM in Lawrence, Kan., claimed WDAF radio was under pressure to hire more blacks when it fired him in 1979. The station gave false reasons for his firing in a letter issued after the termination said G. Stephen Long, attorney for Vaughan.

"Vaughan was fired after the Federal Communications Commission and the Missouri Commission on Human Rights issued a report in late 1978 alleging minorities were under-represented at Kansas City and St. Louis broadcasting stations according to Long.

"A black newscaster was hired to replace Vaughan, according to the suit."

Earshot, a bimonthly trade publication reported: "Another Kansas City, Mo., broadcast outlet is in legal hot water for the way it gave a newscaster the sack. But unlike TV anchorwoman Christine Craft, former WDAF-AM reporter Joe Vaughan does not claim that his age or sex cost him his job. He says he was fired because he's white.

"And last November, a jury agreed with him, awarding Vaughan $175,000 in damages. The decision was based on an 80 year-old Missouri law requiring employers to tell their workers why they're being fired. Vaughan's attorney, G. Stephen Long, says he could also have filed a federal suit under Title VII of the 1964 Civil Rights Act, although the case would have taken longer to try, and, as in the Craft case, the jurors would only serve in an advisory capacity.

"Long told the court his client got the ax because WDAF, a country music station, had no minorities in management, sales or on-air positions and was under pressure from state and federal authorities to do something about it. Vaughan, who had worked in the news department for three years, had the least seniority and was sacrificed. Within 24 hours, a black reporter from another Kansas City station had taken his place.

"Station lawyer Glen Bradford says it was 'only coincidental' that Vaughan's replacement was black.

"He says WDAF made a crucial error in failing to provide documentary evidence of its dissatisfaction with Vaughan's performance. 'With no records, a jury could think this whole thing was made up — which it wasn't, of course.'

"Vaughan says his motive for filing the suit was 'to restore my name. I was a local boy who'd been kicked out the door and given the wrong reasons. I think the court decision was fair.'"

The story was also carried by *The Kansas City Star*

and *Variety*, the monthly international trade publication of the entertainment industry and by numerous
other trade and professional publications.

Several interesting sidelights did come out of the
litigation. It confirmed my key contributions to the
decision-making process leading to a major format
change which rocketed WDAF-AM from a has-been
radio station with what was known as a Middle-of-the-
Road (MOR) format with declining listenership to one
of the industry's most successful country music stations. It has consistently been number 1 in the Kansas
City broadcast market in the Arbitron Ratings, the
Bible of the industry and the rating service ad agencies rely on in purchasing advertising for clients. And,
so overwhelming was the evidence, that the three black
members of the jury voted for me.

WDAF has the best AM signal in the market because it is full time at 5,000 watts and nondirectional
24 hours a day. It's low dial position, 610 kilocycles,
contributes to the effectiveness of the signal and over-
comes some of the interference problems inherent with
AM radio stations.

Frustrated by low ratings and an apparent inability
to take advantage of that signal potential, Taft Broadcasting sent in what is known in the business as a
"station fixer" from the home office in Cincinnati to be
the program director. He was only 22 years old, but
already had an established track record for being able
to rebuild troubled radio stations. I got acquainted with
him as soon as he arrived at WDAF. This guy was a
ball of fire with lots of enthusiasm and big ideas. He
and I hit it off pretty well as we engaged in after-hours
"shop-talk" and bull sessions on how to cure the station's
ratings decline and improve its market position and,

therefore, its profitability.

He seemed to have a high regard for my knowledge of the market and my assessment of what needed to be done at WDAF from the vantage point of a professional who had grown up in the city and worked his entire career there or in adjacent satellite markets. I had no reservation in telling him that I thought WDAF should go to a country music format. I explained to him my reasoning, who to hire to execute it and why that individual in particular would be the person to make it a success. Country music began to catch on with the public across the nation in the mid-'70s and the Kansas City broadcast market was being underserved. The program director was talking to many other people about programming possibilities and alternatives which could be tried as well as doing substantial research to back up the data he was gathering from me and other people he was talking to.

In a few months, he made a decision, developed a plan of action and began putting it together. On February 14, 1977, Valentine's Day, the station officially became "61 Country, WDAF-AM, Kansas City, Missouri."

Obviously, I cannot take all of the credit for the changes made and the subsequent 15 years of phenomenal success that has occurred. However, in a sworn deposition before the trial, the program director acknowledged that he had relied considerably on my advice and opinion in his decision-making process and that I had, in effect, "functioned as an unpaid consultant in the process of determining in which direction to take the station." I am very proud of the role I had in influencing WDAF-AM's incredible record of success!

I won in round two in the Missouri Court of Appeals.

The Associated Press ran this story to all of its newspaper, radio, and television and magazine subscriber/ members:

"A State Appeals Court in Kansas City had upheld a jury verdict favorable to a radio newscaster who claimed he was fired because he is white.

"The Missouri Court of Appeals affirmed on a 2-1 decision a 1983 judgment in Jackson County Circuit Court, awarding Joe Vaughan one dollar in actual damages and almost $174,000 in punitive damages.

"The judgement was entered against Taft Broadcasting Company, owner of the WDAF Station in Kansas City, Mo., where Vaughan was a radio newsman.

"In its appeal, the company contended that the amount of damages was excessive — and that evidence to support the verdict was insufficient and inadmissible."

Taft Broadcasting did appeal the circuit court jury verdict and on May 28, 1985, *The Kansas City Star* reported the following:

"A former WDAF radio newscaster, who claimed he was fired because he was white, had his jury verdict against the station's owners upheld today by a state appeals court.

"In a 2-1 decision, the Missouri Court of Appeals in Kansas City affirmed a 1983 judgement in Jackson County Circuit Court awarding Joe H. Vaughan $1 in actual damages and nearly $174,000 in punitive damages.

"The appeals court ruled that the jury had enough evidence to infer that 'the true reason Vaughan was terminated was to make room for a black, and not because of any inadequacy in Vaughan's job performance.'

"In its decision, the appeals court noted that WDAF's

license was up for renewal in 1980 and management was aware of the Missouri Commission on Human Rights inquiry into employment of women and minorities.

"The court ruled that Mr. Vaughan was never made aware of any dissatisfaction with his job performance and had received commendations by radio management during the three years he worked at the station."

Zealots on both sides of the affirmative action debate made persuasive bids to get my attention and commitment to their causes as word of my unpublicized lawsuit spread. One prominent businessman who strongly backed affirmative action programs chastised me for filing suit because of my family's well-known stands on various public issues and community service. He concluded that, "as a civic leader, you should be proud to 'contribute' to such efforts and drop your lawsuit." On the other side of the coin, I was approached by several people who wanted to use my situation in one forum or another in their attempts to set back or defeat affirmative action hiring programs. I clearly rejected all of these approaches because race was not my motivation; only the unfair process the WDAF-AM management had used to eliminate me.

My OCD symptoms were manageable with low levels of medication throughout this period. (I switched from Valium to 20 milligrams of Ativan per day and discontinued Elixir Alurate in January, 1981.) The positive momentum gained during my years at UMBI in the mid '70s and later at WDAF-AM strengthened my self-confidence and reduced my vulnerability. Of course, there were peaks and valleys of stress as events evolved, but nothing I could not handle efficiently during the course of each day. I had every reason to believe that the worst of my problems had been ameliorated and I was on the road to complete recovery.

The Appeals Court ruling was appealed by Taft Broadcasting to the State Supreme Court of Missouri and, on April 16, 1986, that body issued a ruling in Jefferson City which concluded in part:

"... review of the facts shows that plaintiff made a submissible case and that the evidence was sufficient to allow the jury to infer beyond speculation that the true reason the plaintiff was terminated was to make it possible to hire a black and not because of plaintiff's inadequate job performance.

"Because of this Court's determination that the 1982 service letter statute applies in this case, there is no need to consider appellant's remaining contentions regarding punitive damages.

"Accordingly, this Court affirms the trial court's judgement awarding plaintiff $1.00 nominal damages and reverses and vacates the award of punitive damages."

I never got a penny. But I did get the satisfaction of proving WDAF Radio managers had lied to me and about me and I had cleared my name and professional credentials in the process.

9

Surviving a Trip
through Psychological Hell

Hanging onto a greased vine over a snake pit. That analogy illustrates how hard each hour of each day was for me during a devastating relapse and a series of new OCD symptoms which began in early 1984 and lasted until mid-1988. It was a more miserable time for me than the period between 1961 and 1967 when I missed so much of life. The degree of personal devastation — both real and perceived — was much greater because of my age and what was at stake career-wise. It's alright to exhibit a little odd behavior as a teenager, but 15 or so years into a career in a management position, with employees to supervise and with a wife and child, it becomes an extremely difficult situation. For one thing, it is harder to hide or cover one's symptoms, making the fear of discovery greater. And the possible consequences of discovery intensify the always-present anxiety.

My six years as News Director of Lawrence radio stations KLWN-AM and KLZR-FM were marked by impressive personal and professional achievements.

Personally, April 4, 1981, was a landmark day in my life because Karen L. Reed and I were married at the

Village Presbyterian Church in her hometown of Prairie Village, Kansas. One of my long-standing goals was to find a marriage partner and have a family. I had dated many people through the years, but this was my first permanent relationship. We had dated for approximately two and one-half years before making the big decision to take a walk down the aisle to exchange "I do's."

The idyllic days of the honeymoon were followed by a period where youthful idealism meets the reality of day-to-day living. I can only speak for myself, but I believe every couple soon finds that a certain amount of acrimony is a part of matrimony. No two marriages are ever the same, so it would be presumptuous of me to compare my engagement and marriage to anyone else's. But it was definitely worth doing.

Professionally, a "Kansas City radio voice" doing hourly newscasts on the 500 watt AM daytimer had a tremendous impact on both the station and the community. With the approval of the owner, I completely revamped and updated the news department. The stock market and livestock reports were combined into a contemporary morning, midday and evening package which was renamed Business News. Shorter, more concise reports from the field, shorter copy per story and more rewriting gave the little information-oriented, adult-contemporary format radio station a cleaner, "major market" sound. The Associated Press Radio Network provided a national and international audio service for the first time and effectively supplemented the station's strong presence with taped interviews from city, county and state newsmakers. There were no personnel dismissals or layoffs caused by the reorganization.

The FM station, which began calling itself "Lazer Rock 106," boosted its power to the maximum 100,000 watts and began transmitting from a new, 600-foot tower. News on FM began getting more visibility, too. The improved signal covered the entire Kansas City market and the station did show up in the Arbitron Ratings, although marginally.

The two stations were owned by a father and son, both of whom were prominent civic leaders. With my well-established background of community involvement, I became very active in civic affairs and felt comfortable doing so in the university town of 65,000 people. I was invited to serve on the Salvation Army Civic Advisory Board and later served two, one-year terms as chairman of the board. The Associated Press Broadcasters nominated me to be secretary of the Kansas Board of Directors. I was then elected to two, one-year terms as president of the statewide association. I served on the board of the Association of News Broadcasters of Kansas, the board of the Lawrence Boys Club and the board of directors of Lawrence Warm Hearts, a group of community leaders which conducted an annual fund drive to help needy, low-income residents pay their utility bills during the cold winter months. Over $68,000 was raised the first year from the public appeal. I became a member of the Lawrence Noon Kiwanis Club and served as Chapter Advisor to my fraternity at Kansas University, after completing four years as president of the active chapter's alumni advisory board.

Along the way, I picked up numerous awards and professional recognition including being named "Newscaster of the Year - 1980" by the Kansas Association of Broadcasters and was invited to be Master of Ceremo-

nies for the American Royal BOTAR Ball twice. I spoke
to school groups, university classes and civic groups
around town frequently.

I developed a loyal and talented news staff which
won many individual and group honors for excellence
in broadcast journalism from the wire services and
trade associations. Several people who worked under
my tutelage moved on to fine radio and television jobs
in larger markets.

There will always be one unforgettable night in
Lawrence because it was after I went home for the day
on June 19, 1981, that I REALLY had to go to work!

It had been like any other Friday in a radio station
— very, very busy until after I had left and gone home
for dinner. That's when the day was about to begin
again! Not long after arriving home, a line of intense
thunderstorms developed suddenly with strong wind,
hail, lots of lightning and an extremely odd, yellow-
green murky look in the sky. It had been a warm, sunny
afternoon with the usual summer thunderstorms in
the forecast, but no indication that severe weather or
tornadoes could develop.

As the take-cover sirens sounded, my first reflexive
action was to get to the radio stations. The lights in the
house were out, the sky was that ugly color and I knew
this storm was a bad one and somewhere nearby there
was damage, possibly injured persons and a big, big
story to be covered. My wife was scared and decided to
go with me because we had no basement. We left dinner on the table and ran out the door through sheets of
rain, wind and hail to get to our car.

As we got to within four blocks of the studios, it became obvious that a disaster had occurred. There were
broken trees and debris from homes and businesses in

the area scattered in the street and the traffic signals were out. A little farther on down the street, we could see the AM station's 200-foot transmitting tower was twisted and bent and barely standing. A huge geyser of water was spouting out of the roof of the K-Mart store catercorner from the studios. The other end of the block-long, concrete block structure had collapsed.

Inside the radio station's studios and offices, staff members from all departments began gathering in the customary and mandatory response to an emergency or obvious crisis. It was time for thoughtful action.

Instinctively, I knew what had to be done and began doing it. I determined that both the AM and FM stations were on the air via a gasoline-powered emergency generator, so I ordered the control room board operators on duty to begin simulcasting the newsroom immediately. That is, my coverage of what had happened would be broadcast simultaneously on KLWN 1320 AM and KLZR 105.9 FM. As staff members continued arriving, I assigned them with dispatch to specific locations or aspects of the storm which, unofficially at that point, appeared to have been a small, localized tornado within a line of severe thunderstorms.

I was on the air within 5 minutes of my arrival at the studios. The owner, a man in his 70s with nearly a half-century of broadcasting under his belt, stood at the microphone on the opposite side of the console from me. His son, the general manager, was out of town. The operations manager was also chairman of the city/county emergency preparedness board and had gone to the county courthouse/law enforcement center which was the nerve center for all emergency responders that evening. Other staff members were assigned to the city's hospital, the ambulance service, the fire chief, the police chief, the sheriff and out among the injured people in residences, mobile homes and businesses in the affected area. I coordinated the entire response while anchoring live on the air. One of my first interviews was by phone with the National Weather Service office in Topeka, 25 miles west of Lawrence, concerning the sudden development of the severe weather and how it could have occurred undetected by the service.

As the storm continued it's trek east, it moved into the southwest suburbs of metropolitan Kansas City, some 35 miles away. Knowing this was occurring, I decided to try something on the spur of the moment to get information out to the public after learning that the storm was causing widespread telephone outages as it moved. Miraculously, we were able to get a phone call through to long-time talk show host Walt Bodine who was doing his nightly broadcast on KMBZ-AM in Kansas City, Missouri, about 45 miles to the northeast. Walt and the KMBZ News Department were doing storm coverage and simulcasting on their sister station, KMBR-FM. I asked Walt's producer to let me through to him. Once on the air, we continued to compare notes and trade information for over an hour before the phone connection was broken. Later, people who had been listening said it was interesting and dramatic to follow the storm's path and hear of the events occurring in its wake as they unfolded and the information came in to the respective stations. Walt and I not only talked back and forth but integrated our reporters from the field.

While all of that was happening, we got a second phone call through to the Associated Press Bureau, also in Kansas City, Missouri, which allowed the wire service to monitor the rare four-station simulcast over the telephone and use the material immediately to get the stories out to radio, television and newspaper subscribers in Kansas and Missouri and across the nation. No one I have talked to can remember that kind of cooperative broadcast effort during such an emergency in the region.

KLWN-AM and KLZR-FM were the only local sources of information for the over 80,000 residents of Lawrence and Douglas County, Kansas, about the tornado's aftermath throughout the evening and the early-morning hours of the next day. Public radio station KANU-FM and the Sunflower Cablevision system had no electricity and no back-up energy source for broadcasting.

When officials released the final figures for Lawrence and Douglas County, one man was killed (when the wall collapsed at the K-Mart) and 33 people were injured. Damage exceeded 20 million dollars.

Throughout my career, I always functioned my best when the situation or crisis was the most demanding. This was the pinnacle of many such performances. I was on the air for six consecutive hours with only two restroom breaks and with no medication! Surviving the intensity and drama of that evening without my prescription could not have happened without God's help. I asked for strength all evening in silent thoughts and prayers...and those requests were answered. Never before or since have I been in a situation where I had to come through in the clutch because there were so many people depending on me and no where else for them to turn. Midwesterners are more fearful and scared of tornadoes than perhaps any other kind of natural or man-made phenomenon. I knew all through that broadcast that I had to show emotion and concern yet be calm, reassuring and well-organized as I broadcast the information the many people around me were collecting and putting in front of me on the console. From all sides, I received in the days and weeks that followed tremendous praise for the way I handled a very difficult emergency. The recognition was humbling, but confirmed my own firm belief in my consummate professionalism.

After two decades of steady progress, wretched and inexplicable changes began occurring in my life in 1984.

I experienced more frequent and intense anxiety attacks. New OCD symptoms I had never experienced before surfaced that were frightening and crippling because they were so bizarre. There were many times when I did not know how much longer I could hang on and go to work and do what was expected of me each day. At the same time, I could not just quit. To quit, for any reason, would be defeat and humiliation. Yet, the endless explosion of symptoms and feelings day after day and month after month was ripping me apart.

One of the most significant examples of my convoluted existence concerned golf. I was a different person on a golf course: relaxed, fun to be with and largely free from life's daily burdens. I loved the game and being outdoors. Golf had been one of the few escapes from my father's summer-long fatal illness back in 1966. However, by mid-1984, that all changed. A surge of both frequency and intensity in my OCD symptoms overwhelmed me so badly that I had to give up playing golf altogether. I could not get around the course because various symptoms drained me after four or five holes. I also jogged and used Nautilus equipment during this period, but had to stop because almost any kind of routine exercise would trigger an incapacitating attack.

The three people who were closest to me were of little or no help. My psychiatrist, the man who had literally put Humpty Dumpty together in the 1960s and guided my ongoing recovery through the 1970s, now seemed unable to understand and deal with my "new" crisis. He would unintentionally taunt me during our professional visits with questions like: "What's the matter, you think you're the only guy who's ever been a little bit anxious?" to such lines as "...you wanna be treated like your sick all your life...?" My mother told me: "If your father had taken you to the woodshed a few more times when you were a teenager, you wouldn't be having problems now." The reaction of my wife was equally horrifying and unbelievable as I think back on it. She actually thought my increasingly frequent episodes were all attempts "intentionally designed to control me and get your way" all the time. And, she would stand with her hands on her hips, eyes bulging, and scream at me: "Grow up, Joe. Why don't you JUST GROW UP!!!"

I had no place to turn as my loneliness and isolation grew deeper. If these people could NOT see and believe my discomfort and desperation, how could I expect my friends, coworkers or anyone else to understand? Suicide was no answer and would have been worse than quitting. It would have violated my strong Christian principles and all of the lessons I had learned from my father about persistence and perseverance. My doctor refused to give me Valium, the miracle drug which I had used during my years of rebuilding and personal growth (1965 to 1981). I had to stop using it during the 1980-81 Valium scare and none of the medications that I had used since had been as effective. My only relief came through virtually constant prayer and long, slow, deep-breathing exercises. Much of the time, I felt like I could be taken out by a heart attack or a stroke which, while it scared the Hell out of me, would have been an acceptable escape from what I was going through day after day, sometimes hour after hour.

Specifically, the symptoms that I experienced included all of those listed in Chapter 7 plus the following new symptoms which I had NEVER experienced before: fear of harming others, trouble with violent or horrific images, fear of blurting out obscenities, fear that you will act on unwanted impulses, fear that you will harm others by not being careful enough, fear that you will be responsible for a horrible occurrence, trouble with hoarding/saving obsessions, fear of saying certain things, fear of not saying just the right thing, trouble with intrusive images and general slowness in functioning or delayed response in performing routine functions, easily exhausted or fatigued and general depression. All of my symptoms were explained in detail in Chapter 3.

The difficulty in diagnosing and treating these symptoms stems from the facts that they strike with little warning, may occur independently or co-mingled with other symptoms and do not occur in any predictable order or frequency. A reminder: psychiatrists and medical researchers say OCD victims do NOT act out these symptoms.

I also had an 18-month long bout of Peyronie's disease. Peyronie's disease is scar tissue caused by plaque deposits which build up on the interior walls of a man's penis. Urologists do not know what causes this very painful ailment. The discomfort can best be compared to a migraine headache, except for the location. Some relief was provided by a drug sold under the brand name Potaba. Over the long term, Vitamin E therapy led to a complete recovery. I would not wish Peyronie's disease on my worst enemy.

Shingles, sometimes referred to as "adult chickenpox," is a common and troublesome viral disease. It is medically defined as "an acute inflammation of the sensory ganglia of the spinal cranial nerves caused by a viral infection." My symptoms included groups of blisters about the size of a nickel which would show first near the spine or middle of the back and then spread unilaterally toward the hips near the belt line. Each blister contained a clear fluid which would eventually erupt into an open and painful sore before scabbing over. The feeling is like hundreds of localized pin pricks followed by itching. This process kept repeating itself for approximately six months.

The only treatment was soaking the affected area in hot bath water. This area is almost impossible to bandage and clothing rubbing against the skin caused shooting pains from the sores. It is impossible to lean back in a chair on the eruptions. The shingles sufferer must sleep on his stomach at all times.

Shingles is a miserable illness and, when combined with my OCD symptoms, was comparable to throwing gasoline on a burning fire emotionally.

Many uncontrollable events were happening around me and, in retrospect, were probably at least partially responsible for triggering my relapse. Unprecedented changes were taking place in the broadcast industry by the mid-1980s. The effects of deregulation and the relaxation of other FCC requirements, a surge in satellite programming availability, increasing competition from a variety of sources...all were having dramatic effects on radio and radio news in particular.

When the FCC no longer required radio stations to devote a certain number of hours each week to news, public service announcements, community events and other public affairs programming, many owners and managers sharply reduced, and in some cases eliminated, their commitment in these areas. The new competition and diversity not only divided the audience pie into smaller and smaller pieces, but it thinned and spread out the advertising revenue that stations were able to generate for survival, and hopefully, profitability.

Within the radio industry itself, listeners began deserting AM radio to listen to FM in record numbers because of the better quality of sound and broadcast technology that is produced on the FM broadcast frequencies. The sheer number of radio stations increased markedly as the FCC did away with the earlier restrictions, both technical and political. A plethora of tapes, cassettes and discs hit the market in the '80s. Cable television expanded and improved, led by Ted Turner's highly successful and innovative Cable News Network (CNN) and the controversial Music Television or MTV. The explosion of choices for consumers put AM radio into it's most intense battle for survival since the post World War II emergence of television in the late 1940s.

The first visible signs of erosion came with personnel cuts in large and major market radio stations, usually in newsroom personnel. Many broadcast properties which expanded or upgraded during the hyperinflation of the late 1970s found themselves caught in a squeeze caused by the increased competition, declining revenue and double-digit, frequently 19 or 20 percent, interest rates on loans and other development-related capital.

On the eve of my sixth anniversary as News Director at KLWN-AM/KLZR-FM, September 15, 1985, I was fired. Two days later, the FM Program Director resigned, fearing his head would go on the chopping block next, amid rumors of serious financial problems at the two radio stations. Months later, one of my underlings was named to head the department, but that person's position was not filled in the cutback.

Between 1984 and 1987, I made five serious attempts to buy radio stations in the Greater Kansas City, Topeka, and Lawrence markets. In each case, the owner of the station involved either had "bad books," insufficient records or refused to turn over whatever was available for inspection as a part of the negotiation and sale process. The negotiations seemed arcane and devious. I had been able to get financial backing on my end in two of the proposed deals, but could not get the needed information from the seller. Therefore, no deal was ever consummated.

I felt I would have a good chance of being successful as an owner/investor even though the environment was changing in the industry. It was not polyannish thinking on my part at the time. However, as the depth and totality of the change in the environment became evident by the time the 1990 recession began, I became convinced that it had been a blessing in disguise that none of these ownership situations ever developed.

By the summer of 1990, two of the properties that I had considered were insolvent and off the air and the other three were in dire straights financially and facing an uncertain future.

About the time of my departure from KLWN and KLZR, two men, one of whom I had worked for at two other radio stations, had just completed the purchase of WREN Radio in Topeka from the Landon family interests. The property was in terrible condition. Every aspect of its equipment, sales/revenue, image in the community and the physical plant was in need of rebuilding or replacement. Virtually no capital improvements had been made on the property since 1957.

One of the main goals the owners had was to establish an office in Lawrence which would handle news and sales. Before Governor Landon purchased the station in 1947, it had been located in and licensed to Lawrence, Kansas. My sudden availability seemed to fit right into the plan to restore WREN-AM as a viable operation. I had the professional background and the connections they needed in Lawrence and was a known quantity to them personally from our previous relationships.

It was an emotion-packed decision for me because WREN Radio had been one of the properties that I had considered purchasing. I abandoned the effort after learning the station had an operating loss of nearly $700,000 in one 18-month period when a very expensive all-news format was attempted, but failed. Initially, at least, I had a pretty good idea what these "investors/broadcasters" were getting into, but there was no way I could talk to them about the dilemma they would soon face.

The new owners offered me the position of manager of news and sales in the office they would establish in a downtown Lawrence office building. After much thought, I accepted the offer. It was the only option available if I wanted to stay in broadcasting and not move to the scary unknowns of a new market. Also, I truly believed that, if WREN Radio could be made viable again, these men were the only people who could resuscitate it based on their past record in other broadcast operations, all of which were extremely successful. The Lawrence office of WREN Radio opened October 3, 1985.

The hours were long and grinding and the job more difficult than anyone could have anticipated, even in the worst case scenario. I went to the "satellite office," as it was called, early each morning to check for messages on the telephone answering machine. Then I would go to the city/county law enforcement center for the daily news media briefing with police and sheriff's officials. After checking various city and county offices for news either in person or by phone, I would call the station's main office and studios in Topeka and file my morning update with the News Department. The sales aspect of the job began then. I would make calls to set up appointments with store owners or managers or hit the bricks and attempt to sell time or advertising to Lawrence merchants. Sixteen and eighteen hour days were common. The effort met with only a modicum of success.

By April 18, 1986, I could see the entire operation, including the Lawrence office, was going nowhere. I was taking a physical, emotional and financial beating and could only visualize it getting worse. There were too many stations and a very tough environment for advertising in Topeka and simply no market for the product in Lawrence. I had no prospects for other employment, but knew a talented guy with experience and good contacts would not remain idle very long.

I never did tell the owners what I knew about the

property or that I thought there was no way they could make it work. Sixteen months later and heavily in debt, WREN Radio went off the air on September 2, 1987. The station's final sign-off occurred just ten days before Alf M. Landon's 100th birthday. One month later on October 12th, Landon died quietly at his Topeka mansion.

For many broadcasters, the death of a radio station is almost as painful as the death of a good friend or a close relative. After all, I had worked there two times and had tried to buy it. There was an understandable emotional bond. It hurt to see uncontrollable market forces and financial quicksand suck this old and tradition-rich radio station into oblivion.

10

Many Sharp Rides on an Emotional Roller Coaster Characterized the Road Back

As I scuffled through each day in search of a compass, I knew I was in a psychological holocaust and my survival depended upon my faith and prayer and a commitment to purpose.

The road back proved to be extraordinarily long and winding and the task very daunting. It began with a telephone call to KCMO Radio Program Director, Mike Shanin, and News Director, Jack Ihrie (pronounced like Lake Erie), on April 23, 1986. Shanin and I scheduled a lunch at a suburban restaurant on May 7th to get reacquainted and to discuss the news department at KCMO-AM. Mike was news director at KCKN-AM & FM during my tenure and we had been in contact with each other on and off in the intervening years. He's a friend, a good broadcaster and a quality person.

The broadcasting division of growing media giant, Gannett, Inc., announced the purchase of KCMO-AM and KBKC-FM about this time. This was the fourth sale in as many years for the stations.

KCMO Radio is the Kansas City broadcast market's only nondirectional, 50,000 watt AM station. With a low dial position at 810 kilocycles, the station's signal reaches into parts of ten Midwestern states in the daytime. It's nighttime power is reduced to 5,000 watts at local sunset and it goes into a highly directional broadcast pattern that severely compromises its reach and effectiveness, even within the Kansas City metropolitan area. Prior to FCC deregulation, owners of commercial broadcast properties were required by the federal regulatory agency to hold on to a radio station for a minimum of three years before selling the property. Originally, this rule was designed to control speculation by investors hoping to make a quick buck and to encourage stability in an industry noted for its volatility.

Surprisingly, few members of the public realize that they own the airwaves; that the commercial broadcast frequencies (AM, FM and TV) are public property. The owners of the stations are merely trustees of the respective frequencies which are doled out by the FCC through the granting of licenses to applicants who must meet a variety of stringent requirements. A license has to be renewed periodically and certain proofs of performance must be shown. These factors make broadcasting entirely different from the print media which operate in the private sector without government regulation and whose fate is generally controlled only by prevailing market forces.

Eight days after Shanin and I had lunch together, Ihrie called me with a job offer. I asked for time to think about it and review my career options before making a final decision. The following day I called him back to accept the position. Ihrie asked me to report for my first day on Monday, June 2nd.

He assigned me to work as a producer/writer and to cover public meetings, stories on the street and do general assignment reporting. Then-Vice President George

Bush was in the city my second day on the job which
got me off to a flying start. Initially, I did not go on the
air except in short, prerecorded reports. This was a big
break for me because all of my symptoms had been so
intense during the previous 18 months that I never did
anchor a newscast while at WREN Radio. I was dysfunctional insofar as my ability to handle live air work
during this period. The new situation would allow me
to put the pieces back together, so to speak, much like
a professional baseball player may go through what's
now defined by major league baseball as a "rehabilitation assignment."

Ihrie was an interesting figure. With 42 years in the
business, he had developed the outward appearance of
a gruff curmudgeon. But after he got to know you, he
exhibited a soft heart and was a fair-minded, clear
thinker. He had grown up as the son of a Detroit police
officer, received a degree in English from Indiana University and spent three years in a prisoner-of-war camp
in Europe during World War II.

In the 1985 World Series, the Kansas City Royals
beat the St. Louis Cardinals in an exciting seven game
series. That earned Royals' Manager, Dick Howser, the
Manager's spot for the 1986 Major League All-Star
game. The first public indication that Howser might
have serious health problems was revealed the evening
he managed that All-Star contest. One week later, back
at St. Luke's Hospital in Kansas City, Missouri, Howser
had surgery for a malignant brain tumor.

I was assigned to cover the news conference at the
hospital after the operation. It was as much a technical challenge as it was a personal challenge. I had to
take a portable transmitting unit with me to the audi-
torium where the news conference was to be held.

Normally, this was no big deal with the kind of equipment and the technology available now. The difference in this case involved bouncing an airworthy signal from the portable unit to a nearby relay antennae on a television tower which would send it back to the radio station for transmission and broadcast and do it in spite of being inside a heavily-built concrete, steel and brick building surrounded by all of the X-ray equipment and other interference-producing equipment found in a large hospital. The personal challenge came from being in a new job, in new or unfamiliar territory and from being out of practice because of the dysfunctional period through which I had just passed. I had to overcome the resultant lack of self-confidence. The desire and motivation were there. That part of it was not a problem. Like the earlier-mentioned athlete on a rehabilitation assignment, I had to prove to myself and my employer I could still do the job!

I got set up and everything checked out beautifully. Then, the tension of the countdown to air time began. Back at the station, Jack Ihrie was busily preparing to go on the air with the local news at 4:57, just ahead of CBS Radio News at 5 o'clock. I was communicating with him about the status of the news conference on a walkie-talkie unit through an engineer in the control room. We would interrupt programming and broadcast the news conference the moment it began.

It went like precision clockwork! Ihrie went on the air and introduced me live at the hospital with the latest on Royals' Manager, Dick Howser. I picked up on cue from Ihrie and gave background information about the afternoon-long procedure. While I was talking live, the Royals' spokesman and the hospital spokesman entered the room and approached the podium. I introduced the Royals' official as he began giving a prepared statement, anxiously awaited by the tens of thousands listening to KCMO Radio on the way home from work. It was entirely an ad-libbed introduction. After the hospital spokesman followed the Royals' P.R. person with a medical explanation of the surgical procedure, I gave a summary of the news bulletin as a customary for listeners who may have tuned in late. I closed it out and normal programming resumed leading up to that regularly scheduled 4:57 newscast. At that point, Ihrie came back to me for a recap which was a live ad-lib from the hospital lasting about 30 seconds.

The next day, I got the following memo from Ihrie which is self-explanatory: "Dear Joe:

"Please accept my sincere congratulations and appreciation for the remarkable work you did yesterday (7-22-86) during the St. Luke's Hospital news conference.

"Not only did you pick up the news conference 'live' from the scene, but your comments and assessment of the situation were extremely informative and enlightening.

"I know I speak for the entire news department in congratulating you on a job well done!"

What a confidence-builder the successful assignment and the memo were for me at a critical time when I needed a positive boost so badly. Prayers, indeed, are answered.

On July 30th, the stations' sale to Gannett became official with word of approval coming from the FCC in Washington, D.C. At the same time, it was announced that there would be a new general manager, station manager and program director brought in from other Gannett properties. The perfunctory announcement was made following the sale, "...There will be no personnel changes...," and posted on bulletin boards. Gannett also stated its commitment to retaining a 24-hour news/talk format.

So, here I am: back in major market radio just as the station ownership is changing and the top management is being replaced by the new owner. On August 19th, the newly arrived program director (Shanin became the newsman on the morning drive show) called me in for an exhaustive interview. Talk about cold sweats and anxiety attacks. I had them that day because I knew I was the low man (or woman) on the totem pole and word was there would be cuts. It turned out to be not nearly as bad as I had feared. The new man had a strong news background in some big radio markets. He had been briefed on my professional background by Ihrie and apparently was impressed during the interview. I ended up getting a small increase in salary and assurance that I was in his future plans. Other personnel were either transferred or fired. Whew!! Such interviews between newly-acquainted people are difficult because, by necessity, they are subjective and generally based upon first impressions and intangibles that can be inaccurate at best.

Although I had survived the first round, it became clear that a "slash and burn" mentality or method of management had enveloped KCMO Radio, a management style which often typifies an absentee owner putting his brand on a new acquisition through hired hands who feel they have to make changes whether or not those changes are based on reasoned thinking and planning.

A personal decision Ihrie made caused reason to prevail and bought nearly a year of time for those of us who survived the initial changes and remained under his supervision. The 64 year-old broadcast journalist put the word on the office grapevine that he "planned to retire soon." He was not specific about when, but we knew he would be 65 by August, 1987. Whatever major changes the new management may have wanted to institute in the news department, they would have to wait until Ihrie retired and left. His age, his 15-year tenure at KCMO and the fact he had "announced" his retirement would make his dismissal or firing unwise and unlikely in view of the legal ramifications such a move could have touched off.

A much larger event lay in waiting for me as the dog days of summer faded into the autumn days of September. If I thought my life was in pieces, I did not realize that my soul was about to be pulverized.

On Saturday, September 6, 1986, I got up and dressed to go to a house corporation meeting at my fraternity. I was chapter advisor, was scheduled to give a report and had to be there by 9 o'clock. As I left, my then-wife was feeding my 18 month-old daughter a waffle for breakfast as the child watched "Sesame Street" in her high chair. I stopped to talk to the baby and give her a bite with my fingers. It was fun. A quick kiss, and I was off for the meeting.

The events that would unfold in the coming hours had been camouflaged by the apparent normalcy of the morning.

Shortly after one o'clock, I returned home from the meeting. Tired and hungry, I opened the door to a startling and shocking reality: much of the household furniture and furnishings were gone, so was the wife and no trace of the baby remained. She and her mother and father had cleared the place out while I was at the house corporation meeting, in spite of the death of her father's sister that same morning. Apparently, this was a caper that not even a death could postpone. Within minutes of my arrival, the wife showed up and informed me verbally that she wanted a divorce. She must have been in a parked car down the street, out of sight, watching for me to come home. We had been married for five and a half years.

There are no words to describe my reactions and feelings in the minutes, hours, days, weeks and months that followed except to repeat what a good friend told me who had gone through two divorces. That is, that except for the death of a loved one, there is nothing more gut-wrenching, lonely and painful to go through than divorce.

I would be the first to admit there were serious problems in my marriage. However, my ex-wife had refused marriage counseling, denied me a trial separation and refused any attempt at reconciliation. To add insult to injury, she had slept with me the night before she left me. What happened to me was calculated, cold-hearted and cruel.

This crisis was further exacerbated by the fact my hours were 2 p.m. to 10 p.m., Monday through Friday, and I had a 45-mile commute each way from Lawrence, Kansas, to Fairway, Kansas, (the location of the KCMO Radio Studios) and back. I received considerable support and understanding from Ihrie who had three adult sons, two of whom were divorced. One of his ex-daughters-in-law denied him visitations with his granddaughter, so he felt for my situation with my little girl.

On February 26, 1987, the divorce was final in Douglas County, Kansas, District Court. I was awarded joint custody of my 2 year-old daughter, Lauren Elizabeth.

11

Coming Back Again:
Like the Omnipotent Phoenix

Dealing with the official diagnosis of my illness, a definite downer, was overshadowed by a marked trend toward positive developments in 1987.

On January 30th, Jack Ihrie called me into his office to ask if I were interested in succeeding him as news director. He told me I was the only person on the then-nine member staff who was qualified. Ihrie specifically stated that I had the "attitude, demeanor and news judgment" to supervise a big-time, major market broadcast news operation. My response was that I certainly did want to be considered for his position. He concluded the session by telling me, off the record, that he would retire before August first.

In the weeks that followed, two other staff members who openly wanted the news director's position were told that they would not be considered. One was angered enough by the news to resign immediately.

One of the keys to keeping a job and securing a future in the restructuring of most businesses is to be versatile. Today, all managers are looking for flexible, quality-minded people who can adapt to different tasks without complaining or losing efficiency. It cuts operating costs. I got a chance to demonstrate my versatility by filling in as the traffic reporter for several weeks as KCMO switched from an in-house position, which was eliminated, to an outside service in a money-saving move. In addition, I did sports numerous times in the afternoon drive period when one of the sports guys was sick and again when he was on the road. Ihrie and the program director both noted how smoothly I adjusted to those situations while still performing several news responsibilities.

Purchasing a house in Prairie Village, Kansas, in mid-1987 and moving into it from Lawrence reduced my round trip drive to and from work to less than three miles a day. It was like gaining two hours a day in additional time.

As the weeks rolled by, Ihrie began trading duties with me, meaning that I anchored his afternoon drive newscasts with increasing frequency and looked over his shoulder, so to speak, as he performed his administrative duties each day. These changes had the overt approval of the program director, whose office was adjacent to Ihrie's. He seemed focused on where he wanted to take the news department after Jack retired and I was very much in the picture. I was surprised by the amount of minutia Ihrie had to contend with. During this time period, I was elected to the Missouri Associated Press Broadcasters Board of Directors. And, my efforts on behalf of the Kansas City, Missouri, Salvation Army Social Services Advisory Council were whole heartedly endorsed by Ihrie.

My psychiatrist, Dr. O'Hearne, had attended a number of seminars and participated in discussion panels in mid-1987. Each time he brought back significant new information concerning the symptoms I had and the fact that a diagnosis called "Obsessive-Compulsive Disorder" was being applied to them. As he imparted these data to me during our professional visits, I was more disappointed and depressed than relieved because I knew that, while I might get better and new medications were coming along that would be helpful, I now knew that I would never be totally well.

To his credit, Dr. O'Hearne had always led me to believe that I could completely overcome my symptoms and lead a "normal" existence. Like so-called magic thinking, I truly thought that if I worked and prayed and tried every day, one day I really would wake up and "it" would be gone. Now, I knew that "one day" was not coming. It took me many months to completely reconcile that reality in my thinking. The process was painful. This was a bitter lesson I had to learn. I had to keep going despite my disappointment. There could be no quitting. I knew I had to swallow my hopes and dreams, try to maintain my poise, self-confidence, and public persona and still be determined to succeed in spite of my handicap. I went through a long and sorrowful grief process nonetheless.

Faced with the facts, Dr. O'Hearne began trying new medications that would be more effective in relieving my ongoing symptoms. He never again asked me if I thought I was the "only guy who's ever been a little bit anxious." And, he never again said my pleas for medication indicated "you have a drug habit." Thank God the days of those miserable excoriations were over.

Both before and after the official diagnosis of OCD, I was in group therapy. The effort was largely unsuccessful because I could not cope with the disclosure and dynamics involved in the process due to the intensity of my many symptoms. I stayed with group therapy over a three-year period despite its frustrations because of my trust and confidence in Dr. O'Hearne. But I also grew to understand what poet/naturalist Henry David Thoreau meant when he said, "The mass of men lead lives of quiet desperation."

Jack Ihrie's last day as news director turned out to be July 17th. I did not get his job. A 29-year veteran KCMO newscaster was named to succeed Jack. The new boss was in the twilight of a mediocre career and I placated any disappointment I had by realizing that, if he was 60 years old and had waited that many years, he deserved to cap his career in that manner.

I was named Public Affairs Director and replaced Jack as the afternoon drive news anchor. By applying all of the self-imposed behavior therapy techniques I knew and because of the unusually amicable working relationship with Jack and the program director, I had recovered from the worst aspects of my relapse and was able to fill his shoes in the anchor slot and on the desk. I was using 60 milligrams a day of a new drug called Buspar during this period. Quietly working me into the daily routine slowly over the previous six months enabled me to break down most of the OCD/Anxiety barriers which had made me partially dysfunctional. In the long run, Buspar was not as helpful as the previous medication I had used.

The Public Affairs Director's duties and responsibilities included preparation of five, 60-second public service announcements for airing several times each week. Preparing them involved sorting through the mail received at the station and selecting the PSA items I judged to be of greatest public interest that were being sponsored by or for the benefit churches, charitable groups and not-for-profit organizations in the metropolitan area. There was always more material than there was available time to use it. The copy had to be organized, written and timed because each of the five recordings had to be exactly 60 seconds. 59 or 61 seconds would not do. Each had to be 60... on the mark. I maintained a file of the material which had been used on the air to meet community ascertainment requirements for the FCC.

An unexpected and fascinating opportunity fell into my lap shortly after I assumed the new public affairs duties. Fox Network's highly successful "America's Most Wanted" program with John Walsh began developing localized versions of "Most Wanted" in an effort to expand the concept and help city, county, and state law enforcement agencies capture criminals wanted in their jurisdictions.

The Kansas City Crime Commission developed a "Kansas City's Most Wanted" series for a ten county area in western Missouri and northeast Kansas. KSHB TV, Channel 41, and KCMO Radio were the outlets selected to broadcast the name, physical description and charges against a different wanted criminal each week. The well-known "America's Most Wanted" theme music was used in the background of the local 60 second broadcasts. KCMO Radio aired the public service announcements 20 times each week.

I really got into this assignment and was completely committed to it. It's hard for an active journalist to get involved in a campaign of any kind for any reason because of the many conflicts which can arise. However, this provided an acceptable opportunity for me to get involved professionally in something that would really benefit the public at large. After all, who would question fighting crime, except for the crooks we were looking for?

A lot of kudos and accolades were heard for KCMO Radio's participation in the campaign when the Kansas City Crime Commission held it's 40th anniversary luncheon in late 1989. Over 400 business and civic leaders and representatives of area law enforcement agencies attended.

The Crimestoppers Committee Chairman gave the report for the "474-TIPS Program" during the annual reports section of the agenda. It included a summary of the "Kansas City's Most Wanted" series on KCMO Radio and KSHB TV, Channel 41. Twenty-seven of the 52 criminals featured during the first year, or 53 percent, were captured. The Channel 41 news director and I were asked to stand and take a bow. KSHB TV and KCMO Radio had been recognized by the Crimestoppers' International at the group's convention earlier in the year because of the success rate, one of the highest in the nation.

As the committee chairman was about to end his report, the U.S. Marshal for Kansas asked for the floor. He said that 15 of the criminals on the series during its first year were federal fugitives placed there by his office. He said 12 of the 15 were now behind bars. He said he wanted to "publicly thank KCMO and Channel 41 for their support." There was a round of applause from the luncheon crowd.

When station management approached me two years earlier about being the radio voice of the "Kansas City's Most Wanted" series, I had many fears and trepidations about the project initially. It wasn't long before they had been wiped out after I saw how effective the effort was at helping law enforcement agencies get these scum bags off the street and the tremendous goodwill it was building for the station and the news department among law enforcement agencies and the entire community. The station received several framed certificates of appreciation.

I got a personal letter thanking me from John Walsh and numerous commendations from the executive director of the Kansas City Crime Commission.

On July 29th, Jack did his last newscast and then briskly walked out the door to retirement in Arkansas. The next afternoon, July 30th, I began anchoring KCMO's afternoon drive time newscasts on a full-time, permanent schedule. There was a three minute local update just ahead of the CBS Network at the top of the hour and a two minute headline update on the half hour. Jack was gone, but not forgotten.

The three people with the greatest influence on me professionally have been Charles Gray, Crosby Kemper, and Jack Ihrie.

The weekend of August 29th and 30th was spent moving KCMO-AM and KCPW-FM (formerly KBKC-FM) out of the Fairway, Kansas, building it had occupied with television station KCTV, Channel 5, for ten years into a trendy new office and shopping complex in Kansas City, Missouri's, controversial Westport entertainment district.

The new studio was a disaster from the start for many reasons and, therefore, was a difficult place to work for even the most normal person. Instead of 15-foot ceilings like the designed-for-television structure, we had 7-foot ceilings and the hallways were so narrow that two adults had to turn sideways to pass each other. There was only one bathroom in the studio which had one toilet and no urinal for a daytime average of about 35 people. Every time it rained, a different place in the roof leaked water. It was a claustrophobic and soggy environment.

A restaurant kitchen was located under the news department and, if the cook was frying fish or liver and onions for lunch, that's what the room smelled like afterwards for several hours. Like many of today's buildings, the air conditioning system recycled the old air without bringing in any fresh air from the outside. The humid stench of stale air, cooking odors, coffee, and cigarette smoke was always present. To top it off, the air conditioning system was not built to handle the considerable heat broadcast equipment generates, resulting in frequent breakdowns. The windows were sealed shut, making it a brutal, beastly atmosphere which brought out the consternation in even the hardiest employee. All of these factors were difficult for me to cope with and maintain productivity and efficiency.

The proximity of two nearby hospitals, many cellular phone systems based in the area and other sophisticated electronic interference-producing apparatus resulted in constant technical interruptions with the on-air broadcast receiving and sending systems. Frequent power outages wreaked havoc on the news department's computer system. I remember several afternoons when I had to read the news on the air by flashlight. As long as three years later, many of these problems remained unresolved.

Ever since their arrival in 1986, there had been apparent, major philosophical differences between the general manager, a career bean counter, and the program director over how the news operations should be run. The gulf between the two grew wider and wider until it built to an explosive crescendo. On March 17, 1988, St. Patrick's Day, the program director resigned.

The man named to replace the former program director was an ex-disc jockey from the East Coast who had been programming KCMO's sister FM station, KCPW (Power 95). He had no previous professional experience in journalism, but had been put in charge of a 50,000 watt AM news/talker! The positions, in effect, were being combined in a further effort to save operating expenses and stop the financial hemorrhaging at KCMO.

The matter was analogous to a brain surgeon and a chiropractor. Both have the title "Doctor" in front of their names, but after that, what they do and how they do it have few similarities. Both of these men had worked in radio stations, but that was the only thing parallel about their careers.

One of the first major changes he made was to trim the authority of the news director. It was obvious the news director's position was being downgraded to be more like an assignment editor, if that much. He retained the title, but had little or no authority.

The entire philosophy of the radio station began to change during the summer months. By fall, the pace picked up with more drastic personnel cutbacks.

Again, I had dodged the bullet on the personnel roulette wheel, but I would no longer be News Editor and the PM Drive Anchor. It was decided that a female voice was needed on the sports/talk program. I was assigned to general assignment reporting and put on call 24 hours a day. I did get a station car to drive as part of the new arrangement. The Public Affairs Director's position was also one of those eliminated. I fought hard for the "Most Wanted" series and was allowed to continue doing it on a volunteer basis. The new PD said the very nature of a news/talk format was public affairs so a separate effort in that direction was unnecessary. All things considered, it was not a bad situation for me and I would be able to get out of that miserable building.

I was very proud of what I had accomplished in my 15-month stint as afternoon drive news anchor. The tenure was the longest that anyone held the afternoon news anchor slot during the 1980s. (The lady who followed me lasted only four months.) Coincidentally, the Ed "Superfan" Beiler Show chalked up the highest ratings in that time period that KCMO had achieved in a decade.

It did not take long before the grade card came in on the latest game of musical chairs at KCMO Radio.

12

The Dichotomy: The More My Health Improved, the Harder It Became to Survive Professionally for Reasons Beyond My Control

Radio news is evolving from broadcast journalism where events in a community are chronicled to a new era dominated by what I call the "infotainment boobs."

It is my opinion that the seeds for radio's problems were sown when deregulation began in the 1970s and then snowballed downhill fast in the "go-go" '80s when investments advisors on Wall Street "blessed" the communications/electronics industry as the coming, hot investment. As the money managers, financial groups and conglomerates bought up radio and television stations and other media-related properties, they kicked out the "real broadcasters" and replaced them with accountants, often young and inexperienced, thinking this would assure a quick and profitable return on the bottom line. Each of these poorly prepared, opportunistic insurgents thought he could be the next Ted Turner (CNN) or Mortimer Zuckerman (U.S. News & World Report). It did not work out that way for most of them. Radio, perhaps the oldest and most venerable of the 20th century technologies, took a hit that sent it reeling.

Ted Baxter is not only alive and well, he's running the place now! A scary thought? You bet! But the fictional MTM Studios character seemed to have come to life and taken over in the manner in which KCMO Radio's News Department was being managed. Somewhere in the restructuring of KCMO Radio in the late 1980s, Lawrence Peter's famed management theory, the Peter Principle, appeared to have been exceeded in the constant personnel changes. In brief, the Peter Principle states that a person is promoted upward again and again in an organization until he reaches the level just above his capabilities and there he stays, usually to the detriment of that organization.

After the first Gannett program director with the strong news background resigned in 1988, as previously discussed, I decided KCMO would be the last stop in my broadcasting career. I had no idea how long I could stretch my tenure, but the nationwide trends in the industry and the particularly chronic financial problems and decline in professional standards at KCMO seemed to make the end a certainty. Psychologically, I began preparing for the inevitable. I would not look for other employment or leave. Leaving would be totally compromising my personal and professional principles. And it would be giving up the ship, even though the ship appeared to be slowly sinking. Again, quoting Thoreau: "It is characteristic of wisdom not to do desperate things."

Unfortunately, the mission of serving the public trust with high ideals and loyalty to the community became irrelevant as the accountants assumed control of broadcast operations for a home office hundreds of miles away in another state whose only interest was in the profit and loss statement.

Both the accountants and the far-off home office have no emotional ties or personal interest in the station's "city of license" or metropolitan service area and that callous, could-not-care-less attitude often replaces the original problems the accountants were sent in to solve with new, more serious stumbling blocks.

These non-broadcaster managers lack the background to understand that radio stations are different from almost any other kind of business in that they cannot be successful unless they connect with the local audience emotionally. The "cookie-cutter" decision making processes accountants impose on a business in one city will not work in another in broadcasting unless the local idiosyncrasies of the market are taken into account.

KCMO Radio News appeared to be moving from hard news toward what some call an "infotainment" approach. That is, the information and entertainment are blended using the air personalities or hosts with less and less reliance on traditional broadcast journalists or radio news people. The bottom line is more light stuff, feature news and what I call personality-oriented prepackaged pap. There was a spreading, if unspoken attitude that said, in effect: "God forbid we interrupt our hosts with any real-world stuff... such as homicides, drug stories, AIDS updates, fires, crime news" etc. Breaking news and live, on-scene reports "interrupt the flow of the show, upset people listening in the audience and might cause them to change stations" was one person's thinking.

The ex-disc jockey/program director's philosophical approach apparently was that, if people heard the same thing on KCMO Radio that they saw in *The Kansas City Star* or *USA Today*, KCMO News would sound like it was on top of what was happening in the metropolitan area. This was a radical change. Throughout its history, KCMO had been known for ferreting out and enterprising its own stories, for covering breaking news and for developing new angles and updates on what had been published. KCMO's reputation over the years was that it broke stories before they were in the paper or on television or it was first with the follow-up, new angle on the story or aftermath.

What one person called a "feel-good" format that would not offend listeners was apparently being used to organize each newscast. That is, the already 12 to 24-hour-old rewritten newspaper material or other so-called "sexy" stories were positioned toward the top of the newscast. Spot news or breaking news that had occurred overnight, such as deaths in a house fire, traffic fatalities or a double homicide, for example, were placed toward the end of the newscast if they were aired at all. Overnight happenings had not been "validated" by having appeared in a newspaper first. Often such stories were on other radio stations the day the event occurred, but were reported 24 hours later on KCMO. This approach seemed to reduce KCMO to being merely an audio version of the various local print media and *USA Today*.

Newspapers should be used as resources, as a tip sheet, for background information, a futures file or ideas only. No radio station which considers itself to be a "news station" should rely on newspaper rewrites for its bread and butter.

Some examples of my experiences: One day I was directed to cover a Kansas City, Kansas, City Council meeting during which some heated issues would be discussed involving a proposed landfill in Kansas City,

Kansas. Opponents feared there would be toxic ground water seepage from the dump into a river just above the Kansas City, Missouri, Water Department's intake valve. Kansas City, Missouri, City Council members had threatened legal action to stop the landfill. Instead of being told to (take my 20 years of journalism experience and) cover the story, I was specifically directed to "find some screaming yahoos" and "see if you can stir the pot between the two cities." Written copy would be "lifted" out of the morning *Star*.

One afternoon, the ex-disc jockey/program director came into the newsroom with a waitress he had just hired to work part-time. Her previous work experience was as a flight attendant for Braniff before the layoffs. No journalism experience or anything remotely related.

Another time I was admonished, "We don't care about the story. We just want tape (sound) of the rednecks bitching and yelling." Content and quality were not the objectives.

I was lucky to be with the chairman of the Kansas City, Missouri, City Council's Aviation Committee the afternoon Braniff Airlines announced its September, 1989, bankruptcy filing. One of Braniff's major hubs was at Kansas City International Airport. When I got back to the radio station, the ex-disc jockey/program director grasped the meaning of the story in the tradition of Ted Baxter. Its significance and the role his station had played in reporting it went completely over his head. All he wanted to know that afternoon was "What did Zsa Zsa say today?" ...a reference to actress Zsa Zsa Gabor's numerous court appearances and trial in California following her notorious run-in with a police officer.

After this incident, I decided to write a memo aimed

at educating and enlightening the ex-disc jockey/program director. Surely, I thought, I could wake up this guy and make him aware that REAL news had absolutely nothing to do with Huey Lewis!

The memo said in part: "Approximately 18 months ago, I began the weekly KCMO Radio News city government "beat" in Kansas City, Missouri. I feel it is appropriate to review the effort made during this period in generating voicers and actualities, expanding/extending stories and getting the material on the air in a timely, effective manner.

"Let's look at some of the stories that have helped build a good image and perception of KCMO Radio news: The news team reported on the city's deepening budget crisis during a series of budget hearings the city council held with department heads and managers in March and April. I provided running accounts of the situation as it developed and as the council struggled to make the cuts necessary to balance the budget. Many of these voicers/actualities were on KCMO Radio news hours ahead of TV or in *The Star*...proving there is truth in the old radio newsman's adage: 'Hear it on radio this afternoon, see it on TV tonight and read it in the morning paper!'

"The big break: My first-hand, radio exclusive on the Braniff bankruptcy. I was with Kansas City, Missouri, City Councilman Bob Lewellen when an aide brought him first word of Braniff's decision. Bob cooperated and within minutes KCMO Radio news was first on the air with this dramatic story! After getting a statement from Lewellen, who serves as chairman of the City Council's Aviation committee, I hustled up to Mayor Richard Berkley's office for reaction. (Bob went with me to tell the mayor — exciting stuff!) We protected our own audience, the Associated Press, the Missourinet and CBS Radio in New York City on this nationally significant breaking story. I followed up with detail and incisive reaction from KCI Airport...feeding passenger reaction back to the station in the heart of the afternoon drive."

Frequently, stories occurred that could not be ignored: 1) The 1988 Presidential election campaign brought Republicans George Bush and Dan Quayle and Democrats Michael Dukakis and Lloyd Bentsen to the area. 2) The November 29, 1988, explosion which killed six Kansas City, Missouri, firefighters when they answered an alarm on a construction site. No one has been charged with the murders. 3) Six members of a Kansas City, Missouri, family were killed when their house was fire-bombed in the early morning hours of January 20, 1989, in a drug-related incident. And 4) President Bush's walk through a formerly drug-infested neighborhood in Kansas City, Missouri, on January 23, 1990, to see how a citizen's group had taken action against drug houses. The citizens drove the dope pushers out with nightly marches in front of the crack houses. The demonstrations discouraged potential customers from wanting to buy illegal substances there. The community group then boarded up the houses after they had been abandoned.

The late media mogul, Marshall McLuhan, warned of trends he saw in radio and television news when he said: "REAL news is BAD news."

And, thus, was the dichotomy of life for me. Through tenacity, hard work and the new medication Prozac, I was more able than ever to do my job, but the position was slowly evaporating. I had begun using 80 milligrams of Prozac a day in late 1988. It reduced all of the

OCD and related symptoms dramatically. My overall
improvement was significant enough that the daily
amount of Prozac was reduced to 60 milligrams and
later to 40. I resumed taking 5 milligrams of Valium,
as needed, to control anxiety attacks.

I had the hands-on experience and knowledge of the
metropolitan area to provide the depth and historical
perspective to daily events that define quality print or
broadcast journalism. In an era when life is more com-
plicated than ever and a clear understanding of public
issues so important and hard to find, too many media
outlets have entered a period of cutesy writing and
careless presentation which they falsely believe will
attract larger audience numbers. Superficiality is the
rule. Thoughtful news values and judgement have been
replaced with pandering to the trendy.

Amid increasing amounts of red ink and still-declin-
ing audience ratings, May 4, 1990, became another day
of personnel cutbacks for the management mavens at
KCMO Radio. *The Kansas City Star* reported, in part:

"They may not be extinct but, in Kansas City, the
radio news reporter has become an endangered
species.

"What that means for radio listeners is that, with
few exceptions, what passes for news is either ripped
from a news wire or rewritten from this newspaper.

"Of the two dozen or so radio stations in Greater
Kansas City, only two, KMBZ-AM and WDAF-AM,
have as many as four full-time people on the news staff.

"KCMO-AM, the station that identifies its format as
"news/talk," has only three full-time and one part-time
news employees on weekdays.

"News at KCMO took a step backward Wednesday.
The day the station removed Jerry Fogel from the

morning show, it also fired two full-time news staffers, Joe Vaughan and Amanda Waters. At the same time, it fired two part-time newspeople, Janet Jeffries and Lynne Greenamyre.

"Even before the firings, KCMO did little to gather the news.

"Waters said: 'When I was there, I worked in the morning and all I did was rewrite right out of the paper. Everything I did and the other people in the morning with me, we just pretty much rewrote the paper,' a policy she said she totally disagreed with.

"KCMO's street reporter was Vaughan, who has been in this market nearly 20 years, the last four at KCMO. Vaughan said that, when the Gannett Corp. bought KCMO about four years ago, there were 12 full-time and three part-time news employees.

"There was a time, he said, when radio prided itself on getting the news faster than any other medium. 'Radio has forfeited a lot of that image, at least in this market, of immediacy and covering breaking news.'

"Don Troutt, KCMO general manager, said he had been able to eliminate jobs in the news department through automation.

"The new computer system automatically flags wire stories that deal with events in this area. Another feature is a split screen for employees to call up a story and rewrite it at the same time.

"Instead of going out for news, KCMO news anchors can get it on the phone, Troutt said.

"But there is no substitute for a reporter actually being at a news event, insisted Dan Verbeck, a KMBZ newsman. 'The listeners know the difference,' he said.

"Besides, a radio station that relies too much on the phone becomes an easy mark for savvy politicians and public relations agents in search of a newsgathering vacuum.

"'We're not disguising the fact that we're having to make news coverage economical,' Troutt said. 'We still think we cover the news as well as any other radio station in town or better.'

"That's not much of a claim.

"KYYS-FM does not have a full-time news person. Other music stations, such as KFKF-FM, KLSI-FM and KBEQ-FM, have done away with afternoon newscasts. Last week, KUDL-FM also canceled afternoon newscasts. KRVK-FM never had them.

"Part of the reason is that public affairs programming, once required by the Federal Communications Commission, is no longer needed for a license.

"'There isn't the management support or the ownership interest in having that done,' Vaughan said.

"According to Charles Gray, news director at WDAF, a station needs at least four full-time news employees to handle newscasts and cover breaking news."

I was the News Department's last full-time employee who worked under Jack Ihrie, just three years earlier. My departure brought to an end the weekly "Kansas City's Most Wanted" series on KCMO Radio, although it did continue on the local television station.

So much for the station where Walter Cronkite began his broadcasting career.

Entrepreneurship. That was my career objective post-KCMO. I spent the summer of 1990 collecting information, talking to businesspersons, my friends, friends of my father and attending U.S. Small Business Administration seminars. It seemed there was a market and potential client interest in the sole proprietorship I had in mind.

Even with the great progress I have made against OCD, I need to be in a situation where I am in control of the work load and scheduling. If I need a break, want to get up and walk around or want to work late or start early, I can do it. This maximizes my creativity and productivity and minimizes my remaining symptoms. During the previous four years, I had worked 10-12 hour days which left me too exhausted for much socializing away from work, although I did maintain my court-ordered child visitations with my daughter, Lauren. As a self-employed, sole proprietor, I can set aside the time to be with people and renew and acquire relationships.

So, on October 1, 1990, I announced formation of Joe Vaughan Associates, a communications services firm to be located in Prairie Village, Kansas. The services Joe Vaughan Associates provides for its clients include: corporate public relations, crisis communications, new releases and announcements, consulting-counseling and media training and newsletters designed for either internal or external use. We also provide writer-producer and audio-visual talent services. Joe Vaughan Associates targets small businesses and organizations that do not need a full-service agency and cannot afford to do it in-house.

Civic leadership continues to be very important to me. I am a member of the Civic Advisory Board of the Kansas City, Missouri, Salvation Army and Chairperson of its Metropolitan Social Services Advisory Council, a member of the Board of Directors and Chairperson of the Education Committee for Metro Cancer Action, Inc., a member of the board of directors and the Executive Committee and Membership Chairman for the Native Sons of Kansas City, Missouri, a member of

the American Royal Parade Committee, Indian Hills
Country Club, the Mission (Kansas) Area Chamber of
Commerce and the Colonial Church of Prairie Village,
Kansas.

Postscript

I f the reader were to ask me, at this point, how I achieved my many significant accomplishments in spite of the psychological shackles I have worn, the most honest answer would be: "I don't know!" What I can do is share the formula that worked for me and that I believe would be helpful to many people with OCD.

I will say it one more time: "Don't give up or quit trying!" No matter how big the obstacles may be, or appear to be, continue to press forward with effort and enthusiasm. Secondly, talk to your doctor or minister. Each should be a "safe" figure who will maintain confidentiality. Either one can determine if psychological or psychiatric counseling is necessary. Thirdly, have the determination to focus on developing a productive skill. For me, it was journalism. Whether one desires to be a doctor or a ditchdigger or something in between, make a decision and go for it! And, lastly, use spiritual guidance individually, without a religious leader present. I happen to be a Christian. I believe everyone, regardless of their social or cultural background, is aware of a higher or more powerful being who can strengthen and energize their drive to overcome OCD.

Whatever one's stage in life, it is never too late to pick up the pieces and rebuild for a productive future if there is motivation for change.

For all of our collective complaining and moaning and groaning, we do not stop to take full account of what an accomplishment each day of life represents for the average person. "Normal" lives are hard won because life is war. It really is difficult to earn that state of being that is contained in the daily routines and rituals that are life — a job, family, friends, a marriage. All normal activities require constant monitoring and conscious effort to maintain an equilibrium. The reality of this fact is usually not realized until deprivation caused by OCD, or other dysfunctions, interrupts one's pattern of living.

Inside the civilized structures that are our individual worlds, there is a very fragile balance that teeter-totters back and forth on both sides of the "normal line" as we move through each day. It is not until one falls off of the high wire, as I have, or drifts to the extremes along that so-called normal line, as I have, that one appreciates the routine events and ceremonies of life that most of us just take for granted. It is an unacknowledged miracle that individually and collectively we function as well as we do. Full appreciation of this fact cannot be attained until one has experienced loss of function firsthand.

Finally, there is more hope now than ever before for those who have OCD and similar or related afflictions. You are not doomed if you have the persistence and perseverance to take the challenge of each day as it comes, set achievable goals for yourself and be determined to meet them. For me, the greatest satisfaction and inspiration has come from quiet, simple self-recognition of my accomplishments each day. May God's richest blessing be with you!

# # # # #

References/Resources

For help in finding treatment for OCD, contact the department of psychiatry at a nearby medical school, an anxiety disorders clinic or your local city/county mental health association. The following are additional sources of information.

The OC Foundation's programs include education, research and service to families and health professionals. They publish a bimonthly newsletter and can refer you to a specialist, a self-help group or a professionally-assisted support group in your area.

OC Foundation, Inc.
9 Depot Street
Milford, CT 06460
Telephone: (203) 878-5669

Another good resource, providing the most recently published information on all aspects of OCD, is the Obsessive Compulsive Information Center.

Obsessive Compulsive Information Center
Department of Psychiatry
University of Wisconsin
600 Highland Avenue
Madison, WI 53792
Telephone: (608) 263-6171

Listings of psychiatrists and behavior therapists with a special interest in obsessive-compulsive disorder can also be obtained from the following:

Anxiety Disorders Association of America
6000 Executive Boulevard
Rockville, MD 20852-3801
Telephone: (301) 231-9350

Information on ongoing research in OCD is available from:

National Institute of Mental Health
9000 Rockville Pike
Building 10, Room 3D-41
Bethesda, MD 20892
Telephone: (301) 496-3421

Published information from the National Institute of Mental Health is available from:

Information Resources and Inquiries Branch
Room 15 CO5
5600 Fishers Lane
Rockville, MD 20857
Telephone: (301) 443-4513

ISBN: 0-9636863-6-4

Acknowledgments

Loretta Matlock of Mission Secretarial Services in Mission, Kansas, for her patience in organizing and word processing the manuscript for this book. The Reference Department of the Johnson County Library in Overland Park, Kansas. The Medical Library at the University of Kansas Medical School in Kansas City, Kansas. Station manager Robert G. (Bob) Newton at KLZR-FM/KLWN-AM in Lawrence, Kansas, for the front cover photograph. Retired Kansas City Kansas Community College President Dr. Alton L. Davies who, when he was English-Journalism instructor, laid the foundation for my journalism career. His effort is particularly notable because I had not attended any English or journalism classes in junior or senior high school due to my illness. Professor Emeritus (Economics and History) J. Paul Jewell at Kansas City Kansas Community College who, when he was student activities sponsor, put the first microphone in front of me as the public address announcer at Blue Devil athletic events. And, to the tens of thousands of loyal listeners who heard my newscasts on the radio for over two decades, THANK YOU, one and all!